EARLY PRAISE FOR
THE STREET OR ME: A...

MW00792049

"The desperation, anxiety and chaos of the streets are captured by Judith Glynn in this story of her electric and fraught relationship with a neighborhood homeless woman. As Ms. Glynn bridges that divide by extending her hand, tentatively at first, to Michelle, she depicts the trepidation, risk and ultimately deep connection forged between a middle-class professional woman and a homeless woman. She discovers in her quest for connection something secretly beautiful about our common humanity."

—Kevin M. Ryan, President/CEO
of Covenant House International

"When asked what is the best thing housed people can do for the homeless, many people without a home say 'Just look me in the eye, say hello, and treat me like a human being.' Judith Glynn followed this advice and the result is this inspiring book."

—Eric Hirsch, Professor of
Sociology, Providence College

"An accurate description of the devastation which attends this killer disease. A remarkable love story. Best of all, a riveting read. I couldn't put it down."

—Sylvester C. Sviokla, MD ABAM,
author (w/Kerry Zukus) of
From Harvard to Hell...and Back

Judith
Glynn

the
street
or
me

A
New
York
Story

FOX POINT PRESS
The Street or Me: A New York Story
Judith Glynn

Copy Editor: Mercy Pilkington
Cover and Interior Design: Guido Caroti

This true story is my recollection of events and facts related to the best of my knowledge. All steps were taken to protect some identities. Any misrepresentation was unintentional.

Published in the United States by Fox Point Press
ISBN-10:0-9834595-5-X
ISBN-13:978-0-9834595-5-2

Also by Judith Glynn

A Collector of Affections: Tales from a Woman's Heart

Dedicated to the homeless among us and
to those who will lose their way back home.
There is hope.

Acknowledgments

Books need a byline and words, which are mine here. But a story needs heart. That I share with Michelle Browning, a/k/a Mireille Turoldo. She was a drunk and homeless woman who endured an unimaginable medieval existence on the streets of New York City. After we met, I became as fearless as she was. And for that, I thank her.

Singled out in this book is Dean Albanese, one of my three sons. I'm indebted to him for his support and protection as we returned Michelle to her family in Italy. To my other children, Gregory and Derek Albanese and Lesley Albanese Skeffington, I feel your love every day.

This manuscript was forgotten about until I enrolled in Charles Salzberg's writing workshops in New York City. His expert guidance, plus my classmates' critiques and encouragement, moved this book forward. Bibliocrunch and its founder Miral Sattar provided endless publishing resources to make this book easier to create. Gratitude goes to copy editor, Mercy Pilkington, for her generous help given long after the edit was complete. Thank you to Guido Caroti, a gifted designer, who created the visual to showcase *The Street or Me: A New York Story*.

Many people praised what I did for Michelle, as did she. But many more asked why I went to extreme measures to rescue her. I asked myself the same question then and now. The answers are rooted in mankind's compassion for one another and for walking tall in life. They are gifts that continue to enrich my life and for which I'm thankful.

"Never worry about numbers.
Help one person at a time,
and always start with
the person nearest you."
—Mother Teresa

Table of Contents

Mireille Turoldo
Italy
Spring 1978

Michelle Browning
Formerly Mireille Turoldo
New York City
January 1991

why
bother

IT WAS RUSH HOUR AND A DISMAL February night in Midtown Manhattan. I was on my way home from a temp secretarial job and climbed the subway stairs at the Columbus Circle station. As I neared the top, I heard raised voices and a commotion. The exit was part of the Hearst Building, home to *Cosmopolitan* magazine. Beautiful people were leaving for the day but no one stopped as the confrontation escalated. Instead, they snapped opened umbrellas and braced against the pelting winter rain about to envelop them on the sidewalk.

I lingered to watch two burly security guards shove a belligerent, drunk, homeless woman away from the building's revolving doors. As she struggled against their force, she lost her footing on the wet terrazzo and fell into the guards. Instinctively, their arms reached out to stop the fall before they quickly dropped to their sides. To touch this wretched woman appeared intolerable.

She wobbled for secure footing, only to fall backward and land on the ground with a thud. Her filthy, beige woolen coat and layered clothing underneath softened the fall since she didn't yell in pain. Instead, she spun around and kicked at the men as she lay on her back. Her arms flailed over her head to remind me of a child making a snow angel.

"You motherfuckin' cocksuckers," she screamed, as the guards jumped back.

"Get the fuck out of here, scumbag. And don't come back," one guard yelled as he placed his heavy boot on her ankle to stop her kicks. But she continued to bang his other leg with her free foot. He then looked at his fellow guard and motioned for them to return to the building's entrance.

I was captivated by this woman as the scene unfolded. She was white, approximately five-feet, three-inches tall and thin under her layered clothing. Her long, unkempt, light-brown hair had blond highlights and a natural wave. I guessed her to be mid-thirties, possibly younger. It was hard to tell. Something about her was different from the countless homeless people who littered the city. Her filth obscured a sense of style. She was pretty with a husky voice that carried a foreign accent, one I couldn't differentiate. But it was her translucent blue eyes that transfixed me despite being bloodshot and enlarged with anger. In addition to a large dose of curiosity about her, my feelings mixed disgust with fear of the homeless.

When the guards left, two black men who appeared homeless came out of the shadows. A pungent stench from the trio filled the area, powerful enough for some passersby to gag and cover their nose and mouth. The men bent over to pick up the sobbing woman in the fetal position, one side of her swollen face pressed against the cold pavement.

She stopped crying when she recognized them. She swayed when righted and screamed another obscenity into the air. She then hurled the small paper bag she held in her hand. It hit the building's plate-glass doors, bounced off and hit the ground. The bottle inside shattered, releasing a peppermint scent.

"What you do that for, Michelle?" asked one man. "We gotta get out of here and you're causing trouble again. Damn. We need that schnapps for tonight."

Not answering, she broke into a wide grin that revealed broken teeth. She then linked her arms into the offered elbows of the two men. They guided her away from the confrontation into the dark and wet night. I continued to watch, fascinated by the event, and until the trio hobbled up crowded Eighth Avenue resembling the *Wizard of Oz* characters on the Yellow Brick Road. A refreshing peppermint aroma overtook their absence, as the guards returned to the area with large, stringy mops. With a few whisks and their moans of disgust, the ugly episode and its aftermath vanished.

I'd been riveted by the outburst and had pressed myself against the building to watch, far enough away to feel safe. When it ended as quickly as it began, I opened my umbrella and walked into the rainy night headed toward my nearby apartment building, which was a block away in the sketchy Hell's Kitchen neighborhood. My teenage son, Derek Albanese, was waiting for me to cook dinner. But my thoughts were with Michelle. How did she get like that?

It was early 1989 when I first noticed Michelle in my neighborhood. A rogue atmosphere permeated the Hell's

Kitchen streets located roughly from W. 34th Street up to West 57th Street and from Eighth Avenue to the Hudson River. In the following decades, the neighborhood would become trendy, expensive and gentrified by big-chain stores with a bank on most corners. People would refer to it as Clinton or the West Fifties. But when I moved there, Hell's Kitchen was one tough area where "The Westies" ruled until the end of the late 1980s. They were two generations of Irish gangsters known for murder, theft, arson, extortion and gambling, among assorted vices.

I wasn't a native New Yorker but did own a 400-square-foot studio there for several years. I adored my new home that overlooked a courtyard, a first-time major financial investment for me after my divorce. It had gleaming hardwood floors, sun streaming in and a fireplace that captured my heart. But I was frightened to walk one block over to Ninth Avenue, often littered with discarded syringes used by drug addicts. I was unaccustomed to people who weren't like me and lived in the turn-of-the-century, walk-up buildings. I avoided them. An entrance to Central Park was two blocks away in the opposite direction so I'd head there to see greenery or take a stroll.

When I signed the loan document for my $80,000 studio, I gambled Hell's Kitchen's rough image would improve. What I didn't know at closing when the keys were slid across the table was Black Monday would occur two years later. The global stock market crash decimated the New York real estate market. My studio's value dropped to $25,000, enslaving me to a high mortgage, no resale and a coop apartment building almost in bankruptcy.

My hometown was Providence, Rhode Island, and where I divorced my high-school-sweetheart husband. For the next five years, I lived a dismal and meager life as a single mother to our four teenage children. Eventually, I knew to improve the quality of my life and that of my children's, I had to leave the economically depressed state and start over. My ex-husband happily moved back into the fully furnished house when I sold him my share for a pittance. Several years later, three children remained with him but the youngest, Derek, unexpectedly moved into my cramped New York studio at age 16, failing all grades.

One point during the day of Derek's arrival in New York, I was in tears wondering how I'd handle this unforeseen situation. Surely, my love for him was endless but most people wouldn't undertake a failing teenager under my cramped conditions. I had two closets for clothing, already filled, and a narrow utility closet. My glass-topped dining table was eighteen-inches deep and five-feet long and placed along a wall outside the kitchen, which wasn't eat-in. My bed was a queen-size sofabed, which I'd open nightly. Derek's bed would be a single-size futon chair he'd open into a bed. I purchased a Japanese soshi folding screen to provide a semblance of privacy.

My writing area was a desk and a tall file cabinet against the wall near the apartment's two adjoining windows that overlooked a tree-lined courtyard and where birds chirped. I adored the floor-to-ceiling, aged-brick fireplace that covered half a wall. But with Derek about to live with me in the studio, I could have used that wall for furniture placement, not a fireplace.

As I waited for his arrival in the Port Authority Bus Station a few days before he'd enroll in a new school, I sat on a deserted bench and watched the homeless arrive to bed down in the terminal's dank underground. Derek had never seen people like that. How would he handle New York at his tender age, coming from a small New England city, no father or siblings present and living in a studio with his financially challenged mother? Was I nuts?

"Hi Mom," Derek said, as he walked toward me with a big smile. He carried two, green, plastic garbage bags, one slung over each shoulder, which contained his clothes and his favorite pillow. I sensed his fear when he saw the homeless in the station and about the venture he'd signed on for with me. I splurged and took us home in a cab.

"This is home, Derek," I said, turning the key in the apartment door and opened it wide.

It was impossible for two people to enter the narrow hallway together. Derek walked in before me with a stride, stopped and stared at the one room. He said nothing as I pointed out his one closet and the few drawers I'd emptied for his belongings. That afternoon we went shopping for new school clothes, charging even more to my credit card with its overdue minimum payment.

But it was in the darkness of our first night together and what he said that gave me hope we might make it. He talked about changing his life to make a success of himself. I said I'd help him do it, adding changing one's life dramatically would be one of the most painful decisions he'd face. But he could do it. He would do it. And I'd show him how. What he didn't know or see in the darkness of our room was me curled in a fetal position on my sofabed, holding back sobs and terrified how I'd raise him in New York without child support.

I enrolled him in St. Agnes Boys High School, a small private Catholic high school run by the Marist Brothers and, at that time, located in the East 40's off Lexington Avenue. Derek would be given a chance to succeed but he'd repeat the tenth grade. For the first day of school, I helped him knot his tie. We walked the 20 blocks to the five-story, walk-up school crammed between restaurants and shops. It was a far cry from the middle-class, benign Providence neighborhood with which Derek was familiar.

Whizzing past along our walk were businesspeople with briefcases and joggers on their way to Central Park. Jackhammers tore up sidewalks and cranes hoisted huge machinery above our heads. Two cab drivers cursed at each other. At the outer fringes of Times Square, emaciated prostitutes wearing fishnet stockings leaned against buildings and stared at Derek as we passed.

When we reached his new school, Derek looked petrified climbing the front steps. When he opened the door, I saw a large sign above the main staircase. "The Street Stops Here" greeted my son about to be a white minority, knowing no one except Brother Tom who granted him a second chance. I shook my head, thinking he'd never make it.

Since I despised the restrictive corporate world and was hampered by an eclectic resume that was more entertaining than job landing, I signed up for temp secretarial work. I'd also be hired from time to time for miniscule public relations jobs or to organize special events. The freedom allowed me to accept all-expense-paid trips to write free-lance travel articles for national newspapers. That's where I excelled, but it wasn't a money-maker. My love life was eclectic since I avoided commitment. Eventually, the right man would come along. In other words, to get by in New York, I winged it.

I had sealed my past with no home in Rhode Island. And I'd pissed off a few people along the way. Curiously, I was homeless, too, when I arrived in New York knowing I had to get anchored. But foremost, I had to be a strong example to my children to never give up, to expand their horizons and to never accept how others thought they should live their lives. Tall order, but I'd get it done.

Whenever Derek needed privacy in our apartment, I'd walk our neighborhood and see the same homeless people. They seemed to have territorial panhandling rights at certain banks and corners. The huddled and faceless lumps of humanity were bonded tribal members clustered under cardboard boxes, asleep in bank lobbies at night and hovered in doorways. If Michelle was one of them, I never noticed.

I was repulsed by their ever-growing numbers throughout the city, but my charitable conscience only played out with clothing donations to The Salvation Army. The city's social service agencies, hospitals or drop-in centers could help the destitute.

Derek was watching TV when I arrived home after I witnessed Michelle's confrontation at the Hearst Building. He'd been living in New York for over a year, was doing well in school and worked part-time at a brokerage firm. His tolerance and resilience for New York, especially with our tight quarters, amazed and pleased me. He thrived on the city's energy, as did I. He quickly learned how to take care of himself, particularly since I didn't impose a curfew. The hours after midnight would not only develop his peripheral vision but he'd learn to trust his judgment.

"Hey, Derek," I said, hanging my coat. I'd thought about Michelle the entire time I walked home. I couldn't shake her image or her behavior. "Have you seen that young, white, homeless woman in our neighborhood? She's a bad drunk."

"I don't know, Mom. They all look the same."

"She was something else tonight. I hung around and watched the Hearst security guards push her away from the building. Then she threw a bottle of peppermint schnapps at the glass doors and it shattered. It was quite a scene. I wonder who she is."

"Who cares, Mom? The homeless are everywhere."

"I care for some strange reason. There's something different about her. Oh well. Not my problem. What do you want for dinner? And turn down that TV. I've had a long day. My boss told me I wasn't needed any more. Hope the temp agency sends me somewhere else. How was school?"

<:m:>

Michelle and I were neighbors in a curious way, sharing a neighborhood a few blocks from lovely Central Park. After I first noticed her, I'd spy on her and stand across the street to watch her panhandle. Or when she'd sit on my side of the sidewalk and I'd pass by, I'd strain to hear her mumbled conversation with the same men who helped her at the Hearst Building. I had a lot of foreign travel under my belt as a freelance travel writer but I still couldn't figure out her accent.

One spring night, a full season after the Hearst incident, Michelle was lying spread-eagle in front of McDonald's on Eighth Avenue and West 56th Street. She had passed out, which I assumed was caused by drunkenness. As I stepped over her body on my way to meet friends for a theatre date, I looked down at her toenails poking out from plastic sandals. Chipped, red nail polish covered a few toes. Her shapely legs, blotched with dirt, were visible up to her thighs where a flowered, dirndl-style skirt rested. Her hair fanned out on the pavement and overlapped an empty pint of vodka with its top screwed on. Several homeless men were nearby, asleep on the ground. No one, including me, stopped to awaken Michelle or show compassion to her or the group. Sadly, the growing homeless population and their plight had become a norm for New Yorkers. I was no different than anyone else who ignored them as I traveled on my way to a Broadway show.

There wasn't a pattern or schedule when I'd see Michelle and her homeless companions. In fact, months would pass with only an occasional or distant sighting. Maybe she died I'd think after long stretches and no Michelle drunk or panhandling on my corner. There was no one to ask about her since I kept my curiosity to myself. Derek had little interest if I asked about her.

However, one night I had an allergic reaction to shrimp and waited in Roosevelt Hospital's Emergency Room and heard Michelle's distinctive voice in the hallway.

"My stomach hurts so bad. Let me lie down. The pain is terrible," she said to a passing nurse. "Hey, where you going?" she called after her when she was ignored.

I peeked out my cubicle to see her leaning on a cane, holding her side. There was the slightest odor of homelessness in the enclosed area. If Michelle looked in my direction, I'd close the curtain shut and then peek again. She terrified me at times.

"Give me your arm, Michelle," the nurse ordered when she returned, snapping on a pair of rubber gloves. "Lay down there," she said and pointed to a cot after she'd taken Michelle's blood pressure.

"That homeless woman in the hallway really is an alcoholic," I said to the same nurse when she attended to me. "I see her in my neighborhood all the time."

"She and her cronies are always here," the nurse said. "We've suggested social agencies and detox countless times but some people can't be helped."

"Guess you're right. You've seen it all. But it's a shame. She's young."

"They come in all ages," the nurse said with a sigh.

When I left the emergency room, I passed Michelle snoring on the stretcher. Her long hair was matted. Her face was bruised. A cane rested at her side. An odor of homelessness draped her in place of a sheet. What had happened to her? Did she have a family? She consumed my thoughts as I walked home. Michelle was under my skin.

One early summer evening after another boring day as a temp secretary, I was on my way home and walked up Seventh Avenue near the Sheraton Hotel. My thoughts joined my taste buds as I contemplated what to cook for Derek and me that night. School was finished for the year. In a few days he'd return to Rhode Island for the summer holiday. Both of us needed the break. But my thoughts were distracted by a small group of construction workers lined up across the street. They looked in my direction. There were catcalls, hoots and sporadic clapping directed at several people seated on the sidewalk half a block in front of me.

"Go for it, baby. Lick it good," a construction man yelled, as his companions howled with laughter.

I stopped in my tracks when I recognized one of Michelle's black companions seated on the pavement with his legs spread and a dazed look in his eyes. Michelle was bent over him. His penis was in her mouth. Aghast at the sight, I crossed the street but couldn't stop from looking over my shoulder at her. This stuff was done in shadows. New York was a 24/7 city where almost anything goes but oral sex on a Midtown sidewalk in broad daylight was over-the-top appalling. But who would tell her to stop? No one cared, much less Michelle.

I was deeply troubled that she'd sunk so low. It was an uneasy feeling to care what Michelle did and to feel embarrassed for her. I didn't know her, much less want to, but I had to know more regardless of her lewd behavior. The larger question was why I was fixated on this woman.

The opportunity to confront my fascination with Michelle came several days later and at the same spot on Seventh Avenue. I noticed she was alone and seated on the sidewalk. Her cane rested across her knees. We locked eyes as she shook a cup with jingling change and raised it as I approached. She appeared sober, cleaner than usual and sweet. There was a jittery beat in my soul. I stopped.

"Can you spare some money?" she begged.

"I've watched you for six months. You're always in my neighborhood. Your name's Michelle, isn't it?" I said feeling propelled to talk to her.

A beguiling grin crossed her bruised face at the mention of her name. "My name's Mireille, but people can't say it so I say 'Michelle.' It's Michelle Browning."

"Mireille? I never heard that before. How do you spell it? And where do you come from?"

"I'm from Coderno di Sedegliano in Italy. My parents are Italian but I was born in Dijon, France when they lived there. My name in Italian is Mariella but I spell it the French way."

"How can your name be Browning if you're Italian?"

"Because Steve Browning is my husband."

"Is he one of those black guys I see you with?"

"No! My husband is white and comes from Kentucky. He's across the street working."

Astounded by her words, my head jerked to look in that direction. I saw a white, dark-haired, bearded man, slightly stooped, balancing himself with a cane and begging with a cup. I'd seen him before sitting with her on the sidewalk. She'd put her head in his lap many times. What a racket, I thought, husband-and-wife panhandlers. I wanted to mention the street oral sex she'd performed on a man who wasn't her husband but wondered if she'd even remember, so I let it slide.

"How long have you been on the streets?"

"I don't know. Six, maybe seven years."

"How old are you?"

"I'm 33."

"Do you have a family?"

"Oh," she answered, as the child within sprang to life. "You should see my family. They're rich. My mother, sisters and brothers live in Italy. But they don't know I live like this. My mother writes to me using the church's address. I call her collect."

"Do you want to change your life?" I blurted out. "I might look like a fancy lady but I've seen hard times. It's possible to change. Want to try?" I knew it was absurd to jump in and offer my help but I felt I had to do it even though I knew nothing about homeless drunks and recovery.

"Maybe."

"I'm not a social worker, but I'll research rehab possibilities for you and Steve. This is no life for a woman."

"I'll think about it," she said.

I knew my words were familiar. I also knew the power of an addiction. Death isn't something an addict thinks about; the dependence is strong. As a well-dressed man approached, complete with briefcase and polished shoes, Michelle interrupted our conversation to panhandle from him.

"Got any money?" she asked me again when he refused.

"No money. Next time we'll have a longer talk. My name is Judith. Don't forget me," I said, experiencing relief because I'd finally spoken to Michelle, the woman who haunted me.

When I walked home, I chastised myself for not chastising Michelle for the shameful oral sex act she'd performed in public. If I saw it again, I'd remind her how to be a lady, even in the gutter.

⟨ːmː⟩

Alcoholism was a disease, or a choice, I knew well. I was five when my mother divorced my alcoholic father because of it. He wasn't in my life as I grew up. Several members of my Irish family drank too much or were in recovery. But no drunk I knew was in the gutter year after year. Nor was I naïve to think Michelle could be forced into recovery; that decision was hers.

After our first hello and whenever I'd leave my apartment building, Michelle Browning became my neighborhood focus. If she were across the street, I'd cross to greet her. If she were propped up against a building, I'd bend down to exchange pleasantries. She was always polite, and her warm smile lit up the sidewalk whenever I approached.

One fall day on Eighth Avenue, months after our formal hello, Michelle was again stretched out on the sidewalk. This time her eyes were closed. Several homeless men sat nearby and watched as I shook her shoulder to awaken her. That day I didn't want to pass by without acknowledging her, asleep or awake. Maybe she needed food.

"Hey, Michelle. Wake up. Did you eat today? I can go to the deli for you."

"Hello, Judith," she said, as her eyes opened slowly to meet mine. "I'm dying. I won't make it through the winter on the street," she continued, as her voice dropped to a whisper.

"I know you're dying, Michelle. You have to stop drinking. Work with me to change your life." She passed out before I finished my plea. I looked at the homeless men who simply nodded their agreement. Frustrated and clueless about what to do next, I stood up and walked away. I sensed their eyes on my back.

Michelle encounters were happenstance. When I hadn't seen her for a while, I'd ask the corner grocer about her. She and her gang were constant pests, either stealing ice from the bins or food from the outside area. One day, he said she'd been beaten and taken by ambulance to Bellevue Hospital. Oddly, I felt driven to visit her and questioned my sanity at the East 23rd Street subway stop where I purchased a bouquet of flowers and two candy bars for my visit.

Bellevue Hospital dates back to 1736 and covers several blocks along First Avenue in the East Twenties. The large brick buildings house hundreds of patients and employees. When I entered the main building, I saw a cordoned-off waiting area and a manned police cubicle off to the side.

"Is Michelle Browning a patient here?" I asked the clerk at the reception desk.

"Room 1612," she read from a computer screen. She then asked for my ID, wrote my name in a large book and handed me a Visitor sticker. I felt like a member of Michelle's family when I stuck it on my lapel. But would Michelle allow me in her room when she saw me? And what was I doing at Bellevue visiting a homeless woman? This was crazy.

A bloodied rubber glove was in the corner of the elevator when I stepped in and rode it to the 16th floor. As I walked the long corridor to Michelle's room, I glimpsed in cavernous rooms, each with four beds and all occupied by wasted bodies. Some rooms had peeling paint and were devoid of decorations. The roar of traffic could be heard through large windowpanes.

As I approached Michelle's room, she stood outside it, talking with one of the black homeless men she'd sit with on the sidewalks.

"How you know I'm here?" she asked sweetly as I neared her.

"Oh, you'd be surprised. Let's go in your room and talk," I said and handed her my gifts. The homeless man with the hat pulled down to his nose slinked away. That day, Michelle wore a hospital gown tied at her back, which accentuated her distended stomach, typical of acute alcoholism. Her oversized, foam rubber slippers exposed swollen ankles. A long scab covered her nose.

"How did you get that sore?" I asked.

"A transit cop beat me," she said matter-of-factly. "These flowers are pretty," she added and shoved them into her bedside water pitcher after she crumpled the wrapping paper and threw it on the floor. The blooms gave her corner of the room a touch of class.

"Want some soda?" she asked and reached for a covered cup on the nightstand. "Don't worry, I haven't touched it," she added.

"I'm concerned when I don't see you around," I confessed after refusing the soda.

"I'm sleeping in bank lobbies or in subway stations or panhandling on the streets or passed out. Sometimes I sleep in the park. Steve tells me it's like camping out," she added with a chuckle. "What have you been doing, Judith?"

I hesitated. Should I be truthful? I was preparing for a press trip to Portugal and would be gone ten days to research material for my monthly travel shopping column in the *Chicago Sun-Times*. It was great for byline credits and the $150 the paper paid went toward my son's tuition. All travel expenses were paid by the Portuguese government, but I still had to work my temp secretarial jobs to manage finances.

"I'm going to Portugal for a week to research and write travel articles," I said, feeling guilty for my good fortune.

"I miss Europe and my mamma's Italian cooking. But I'd never live in my town again, not after being in America."

"How did this life happen to you?"

Slowly, and with a faraway look, Michelle said her American dream began when she was 19 and she was crowned Miss San Daniele, a distinction of honor in her northern Italian town. When she met a Houston journalist and his wife in a Venice bar, he promised a modeling career in America. Michelle was packed in no time, even though her family disapproved. According to her, the journalist tried to seduce her when his wife went to the hospital to deliver their baby. Michelle ran away from their home but stayed in Houston where she met Steve Browning, her future husband.

Supposedly, he came from a well-to-do Kentucky family, which financed their expensive home, eventually lost to debt. Steve worked as a glazier but drinking and drugs were an everyday event for them. She revealed he drank from the age of nine. She drank in Italy, but not as much or as early. Their trail from Houston to the streets of New York was littered with occasional jobs, fun, money, drugs, booze, trouble, unpaid bills, beatings, failed attempts at rehabilitation, countless emergency rooms and charity wards, sleeping in subway stations and street horrors.

"You had to know life was going downhill for the both of you, Michelle," I said, stopping her before she could continue with details from their sordid life.

"*All you need is love, dom, de, dom, dom, dom,*" she sang. "Like the Beatles, Judith?"

"Very funny. Sure I do. So what happened to you and Steve in New York?"

"When we arrived, we lived in the Henry Hudson Hotel on West 57th Street for a while. I loved to parade down the street, all tight-assed in my mini-skirt and high heels. I wasn't a hooker," she said before I asked. "I was drunk and high on drugs. I admit to that. And I was a go-go-dancer in the Kit Kat Lounge on Seventh Avenue. Made a lot of money but Steve and I drank it away."

"Did you ever look for other work?"

"I tried but when you sleep in the park, can't shower and wear the same clothes, no one would hire me. Steve couldn't get a job either. You met Steve. Remember him, Judith?"

"I do."

She'd introduced us one day when I stopped to acknowledge her. Although complacent, friendly and still handsome, Steve seemed demented. He couldn't follow a conversation and nodded off repeatedly. Michelle's deep love for him was obvious, even from a gutter view. I knew I'd have to work around or through Steve if I wanted to reach her. There was no way she'd leave him for rehab or a future alone.

"Do you ever daydream about a better life?"

"I stopped daydreaming when I ended up on the street. I'm dying, Judith. How can I make it through the winter?"

"I don't know, but die with dignity, not in the gutter. Want to go home to Italy?"

Tears formed. "If my mother knew the truth, she'd yell. Look at me with missing teeth and a broken nose." She parted her hair saying clumps had been pulled out during fights.

"When was the last time you saw her?"

"I don't know, maybe three years ago. My father died last year. He spoke 21 dialects. I speak five languages. *Parlez-vous Français?*" she asked with a touch of elegance in the charity ward.

"And no one has come to see you in New York?" I ignored her boasting.

"My cousin Paolo came once. He's maybe 19. I use a guy's address in the West 50's. His name is Eddie Benson. Paolo went there looking for me, and that guy took him to the Columbus Circle subway station where I was panhandling. Paolo burst into tears and asked why Steve wasn't caring for me. Maybe he didn't tell my family when he returned to Italy because no one said anything."

Michelle was one of six children. Her Italian-born parents moved to France where her father supervised building projects. She was 11 when the family returned to Coderno di Sedegliano, a village northeast of Venice. The culture moves accounted for her ability to speak French and Italian fluently. She said she had three years of college and a hairdresser's license. As the stories grew, I couldn't decipher truth from hallucination. And why did I care?

"Do you have a family?" she asked.

"I'm an only child and come from divorced parents. I'm divorced, too, and have four children. One son lives with me in New York. Two others and my daughter live in Rhode Island with their father. I'll show you pictures someday."

"And I'll show you my family photos. You'll be surprised."

"I'd like that, but I have to go," I said, as I stood up. I'd run out of topics. And why was I there? Had a writer's curiosity brought me to her room? "See you in our neighborhood. Think about sobriety, Michelle. I'm clueless how to help but I can try."

"I'm not interested in a fuckin' do-gooder."

I'd never been called that before. But as I prepared to leave, I faced a dilemma. Should I hug her? Did she have body lice? Would they hop on me? Do I kiss her on the cheek? Just how far did my compassion extend? Or was I a societal voyeur getting kicks out of her misery?

Judith Glynn's family in 1989 when she met Michelle Browning.
(Left to right) Dean Albanese, Judith Glynn, Gregory,
Derek and Lesley Albanese.

In the hospital hallway, Michelle wrapped her arms around me and kissed my cheek. She thanked me for coming and said the flowers and candy were the perfect gifts.

I hugged her back, walked away with a wave and felt itchy all over. On the long bus ride home, I wondered what I could do for Michelle Browning. Alcoholics are superb manipulators. They keep people trying to help as they continue to drink.

"I'll never go to those shelters," she told me often. "They're hell. I prefer the street."

The next day, I called a Bellevue Hospital social worker. Michelle had a long record at that hospital, too. Same message as the one I heard at Roosevelt Hospital. There was little anyone could do until she voluntarily checked into a detox unit. Several days later, I returned to Bellevue to visit Michelle, again with flowers and candy bars in hand. But she'd checked out using a West 50's address. Eddie Benson had signed the release form. Disappointed and discouraged, I left the flowers and candy at the nurses' station. During the bus ride home, I decided to let Michelle die in the gutter if that was her fate. I was done with my Florence Nightingale role. I had my life to live, my son to care for in the city, other children needing me and serious money had to be made soon.

i'll be your friend

WHEN 1990 ROLLED AROUND, I'D BEEN talking to Michelle for about a year. I couldn't stop. She'd be languishing on a sidewalk in my neighborhood or in a subway station. I'd say a quick hello, maybe bring along a sandwich and remind her about sobriety while she ate it. She'd assure me she'd *think* about it. Steve was usually close by, looking worse by the day. He'd say hello if he could focus on me.

I kept my travel articles going month after month, still not making much money, but I saw the best of Mexico, Quebec, France, Australia and other destinations. A fantastic travel-writing perk allowed me to take my children along on some trips if my companion's air fare was paid. Since my eldest son, Greg Albanese, was petrified to fly, I thought the best way to squash that anxiety was a trip to Australia. Eight flights in all and he conquered that fear.

The next child who needed a break out of a small-town mold, at least in my mind, was my daughter Lesley Albanese. By 20, she was tall and beautiful with olive skin and brown eyes. She was also falling in love with her future husband and working as a secretary in Providence's City Hall. She lived at home where she'd acquired a terrific sense of humor as the only female in the house with a father and her brothers. She had a resilience I didn't see in her friends; the rare combination of an innate shyness reinforced with a steel spine. We were close. We were friends. But I knew my role was to be a guiding light, not her buddy.

We talked by phone, almost daily, and I visited Providence enough to satisfy the guilt others placed on me because I wasn't around my children full time. But, unlike my sons, Lesley didn't have a sense of adventure.

"It's time to travel outside your comfortable world," I said to her one day.

"I don't have that much interest, Mom."

"That's because you haven't been anywhere. You need to experience a new culture. It's another form of education to struggle with a menu in a foreign language. Get lost in a strange country. I've done it all and want you to experience challenges so you can judge whether you want to travel or not. I'm writing travel articles about Spain and Portugal next month. Let's go. And don't you dare say no."

Since Madrid, Spain was a favorite place of mine, we went for long walks along sweeping avenues with Baroque, Renaissance and Gothic buildings, many bedecked with wrought-iron balconies. Block after block was intersected by fountains that spouted water into the sunshine. We took three-hour lunches, complemented with wine, and followed by a long siesta.

"It's our one contribution to the world," quipped the hotel clerk when we asked about the custom. "We're always so tired in this country because we stay up too late."

I introduced my only daughter to the *paseo*, which is the customary early-evening stroll done for hours by Spaniards. Lesley had never walked more than a few blocks in Providence, especially with a car in the driveway. "Spaniards stare at everyone just a little longer than you're used to," I warned. "Just stare back."

No visit to Madrid was complete without showing her the *Plaza Mayor* in the city center. Its rectangular shape dates back to the mid-16th century. Several stories above contain apartments with hundreds of balconies where Spaniards once watched the canonization of St. Theresa, the beheading of the Prince of Wales and the burning of witches. Confessions were commonly heard before bullfights. There were dozens of cafes with outdoor seating and where Lesley and I pulled up a chair.

"How's Derek doing in New York, Mom?" she asked me that day over *paella* in a Madrid restaurant. Only 18 months apart, he looked up to his sister. "Looks like he's not coming back to Rhode Island," she surmised.

"He's doing great in school, has good friends, an after-school job and will probably enter the financial field after college. Keep calling him, hon. He loves you a lot. Hey, did I tell you about Michelle, the homeless woman in our neighborhood? I can't stop talking to her."

"What's the attraction?"

"I can't put my finger on it. She's charmed me in an odd way. My God, how can anyone be homeless for six or seven years and still live? She's so dirty, smelly and drunk. Maybe I want her to have contact with a woman like me who says hello."

"Be careful, Mom. I know you like to help people when they're down. Or you like to pitch in but you end up doing too much. I remember the school's bake sales you organized, helping the principal start a kindergarten, helping on political campaigns. You're very success-driven but homelessness is new for you. What does Derek say about her?"

"At first, he was disgusted. Then he'd see the crazy stuff she did and call me from the street to report her antics. Watching this medieval culture fascinates both of us."

<cm>

In spite of my declaration to myself and others that I wouldn't talk to Michelle because there was little I could do to help her, that claim faded one day in the summer of 1990. As I passed, she wanted to introduce me to the homeless men in her pack. They seemed grateful for contact with a society that ignored them.

Philip, a bearded, 40-something and handsome black man, was tall and slender. He eyed me suspiciously and pulled his hat down. He was the man I saw outside Michelle's Bellevue Hospital room. His foul odor was overpowering.

"Hi Philip," I said, trying to sound friendly. "Where do you come from?"

"His family lives on Long Island," Michelle answered.

"This is Muskrat," Michelle said, as she pointed to a short man with watery blue eyes and wiry salt-and-pepper hair, worn shoulder length. He was around 50. Even seated on the ground, his legs bowed. His pants were stained with urine. One leg below the knee was wrapped in pus-stained gauze.

I'd seen him around. Sometimes he'd sing Irish ditties while seated against a building. His badly infected leg had to be dressed at the hospital; otherwise the stench from the dead, rotting skin was putrid. Michelle told me the other homeless refused to let him sleep with them in the bank's ATM lobby. In the summertime, between his rotting leg and his wet pants, flies landed on him.

"Muskrat? How'd you get that name?" I tried not to gag.

"They gave it to me," he said. "My name's Paddy Lynch. Nice to meet you, Judith."

Eugene was a burly, round-faced, red-eyed, 40-something black man. Michelle said he'd left a girlfriend and four children on Staten Island five years before. Sometimes he cleaned up at his sister's home.

"Can I hug you?" he asked and walked toward me.

"Not today, Eugene," I said and took a step backward. "But you better be careful. I've been a divorced lady for several years and I'm looking for a new guy. You might be him, but you've got to clean up before I kiss you."

"And you've met my husband, Steve. He has meningitis," Michelle said as she looked his way. But Steve had already passed out when she acknowledged him.

Michelle was holding court on the sidewalk. Was I watching the ultimate party, a group with few worries? Of course, there was the possibility they'd freeze at night but they conquered that challenge by huddling in bank lobbies and on subway platforms. Money wasn't a big problem. Michelle was a master panhandler. When the men failed at handouts, she'd go barefoot, stagger more than usual and plead. Within minutes, she'd have cash for the liquor store.

"I don't care about money," she once told me. "Philip had an accident in his sober days and the insurance company gave him a $1,000 a month for his lifetime. We go to a downtown bank every month to collect it. But that bastard made a pile out of the money one day and lit it. He wanted to keep warm. Now I'm his treasurer."

"How do you keep the money safe?"

"I'm petrified to be left alone. Those motherfucker street people know about it. Sometimes I roll ten one-hundred-dollar bills in cellophane and put them in my pussy."

"I'll remember that next time I touch a $100 bill."

"You just never know where it's been now, do you Judith?"

<m>

Michelle, Steve, and their vagrant pals always had a problem. The police would beat or hassle them. The hospitals employed mean doctors and nurses. Social agencies were useless. Everyone was at fault but them. I'd listen and then put the responsibility of others' behavior back on their behavior. My words fell on deaf ears. The only progress I gained moving Michelle toward sobriety was her smile that grew wider when I'd approach. My friendship was invaluable to her. I decided to stay around a little longer.

"How are your children?" she'd always ask.

"Everyone's fine. My oldest son, Greg, is becoming a crane operator. Dean is a carpenter and Lesley bought a new car. Derek loves New York."

"Can I meet them some day?"

"Maybe. Do you have any women friends?"

"Nope."

"I'll be your friend."

"Judith, look at me. I'm dirty. I get things at the church but you dress better than what they got. Can you bring me clothes?"

I went home and returned with a light-weight pink jacket. She wore it for weeks. I bought her a book with inspirational sayings. It was stolen that night. Trying to help her led me to wonder how I'd put my support into practice. Would I accompany her to AA meetings? I'd done that with an alcoholic cousin and was bored stiff. She continued to drink until she sobered up on her own. Maybe I could find a women's shelter to accept Michelle. Taking her to my home made me uncomfortable and fearful. Another reality for me was that I'd grown bored and weary with dropout conversations and habitual drunkenness. Homelessness was horrible, but all I could do was be kind to Michelle. She'd have to find her own way out. So as my life became busier, I saw less of Michelle and didn't seek her out as much.

❧m❧

On a sweltering summer day, I saw Michelle staggering on Eighth Avenue at my corner of West 56th Street. She was barefoot. Her sleeveless blouse was opened far too low, which exposed her sagging breasts. She was disheveled more than usual with a wide gash over her left eye. I watched as she purposely bumped into people.

"Come on," she'd slur and extend a cup. "Gimme some money. I need money now."

As usual, streams of people ignored her or stepped aside, repulsed. When I approached, she dropped her hand with the cup in it and walked beside me.

"You're drunk again, Michelle. When will this stop?"

"Steve died yesterday at three o'clock," she wailed.

"Who told you that? Are you sure?"

"He died at Bellevue."

"I need to verify this," I said and walked to a nearby payphone. Street life was full of misconceptions. Was this another one? Reality was so clouded for Michelle, she'd believe anything.

"Bellevue Hospital. Can I assist you?" the operator answered in a sing-song voice.

"Could you please tell me if Steve Browning passed away recently at your hospital?"

There was a short wait until the operator said matter-of-factly, "The computer does not show that he expired."

What a clinical response, I thought. "He didn't die," I said to Michelle, cupping the mouthpiece as I looked straight into her blood-shot eyes. "The operator said he didn't expire. He's alive." By now passersby gawked at me, disgusted I'd associate with Michelle who swayed from side to side.

She stared at me. She gasped. She blinked as if trying to sober herself. She grabbed the telephone from my hand. "What? He expired?" she screamed at the operator who probably wasn't on the line anymore. She banged the receiver against the payphone cabin, crying hysterically.

"No. He didn't expire. He's alive," I said but a fire truck raced by and drowned out my words.

Michelle thumped the payphone cabin with her fists. Several people stopped to watch our spectacle.

"He's alive, Michelle," I shouted and clenched her flailing hands. "Would I lie to you?"

She shook her head no. We were like schoolyard chums professing loyalty and friendship on that street corner.

"He didn't die. Believe me. He's alive, Michelle," I said softly but wondered for how long.

She suddenly perked up. "Buy me a fucking hamburger," she demanded and staggered out into the approaching traffic. One cab narrowly missed her.

"Christ, watch where you're going. You'll get hit. Then you'll die and Steve will live," I said over the traffic noise. I followed her to McDonald's where I purchased her order. "Let's sit here," I said outside and led her to an apartment building's steps. "Come on, Michelle. Time to sober up. Let me help you change your life," I pleaded while she ate.

"I'll think about it," she answered and gulped her Coke after stuffing a handful of French fries into her mouth. "And thanks for finding out about Steve. I trust you, Judith."

When I left her that day, I again vowed to myself I was through helping Michelle. How could I rescue her? She was too far gone. But despite that declaration to myself and others that I was through with Michelle, I continued to talk to her on the street and anywhere else I saw her.

‹ːmː›

In the fall of 1990, I was in a funk for weeks when the leaves turned brilliant colors and fell softly over my beloved Central Park. Derek had entered Northeastern University in Boston, MA and was gone from our little apartment. But I knew he'd return to live in New York, which was home, and go off on his own.

I was realizing with Derek gone that I hadn't taken care of my love life. There was no significant man in it. But, then again, who'd want me crossed my mind often. I believed there were no men in New York who'd take on the responsibility of part-time stepfather to four teenagers, especially when finances were stretched across my broken family. And I didn't want to be a stepmother to someone's children either. My fate for a lifelong companion, at that time, seemed dubious.

One night, I resorted to a walk up Broadway and into the Upper West Side. I wanted to rethink my life's direction, man or no man in it. Leisurely steps always cleared my mind, which they did that night, but I still carried an overwhelming loss with Derek's spirit now gone.

On my way home, I must have had a blank, distraught face, similar to those of the homeless I'd seen for years. When I reached the Chase Bank at Columbus Circle, I instinctively looked inside the lobby. Michelle, Philip, Eugene, Steve and an odd, frail man dressed in black where there. All but Steve, who was a lump of a body seated in the corner, were dancing. The man dressed in black held a portable cassette player with a handle. He swung it back and forth. Fast dance music came from it. Everyone jumped about, arms held over their head, similar to a tribal dance for its members.

Michelle glanced at the bank's outside window and saw me looking in. She stopped dancing. She waved and smiled. I didn't wave back. She stared at me, a woman in the shadows, looking back at her. Her smile turned to concern as she walked over to the door and opened it.

"Something's wrong. I can see it. What happened, Judith?"

"I'm sad tonight. Derek left for college, and I realize there's no man in my life to love."

"Your kids can take care of themselves. Find someone who will love you like Steve loves me," she said and gestured his way. But he'd passed out and didn't return her praise.

"I know, Michelle. I know but you don't understand what it's like to be responsible for children. Don't judge me for not having a man. Maybe he'll come along some day."

Michelle moved closer and hugged me, as I began to cry.

"Marie, come back and dance for us," Philip called over to her. "Hey, Judy, how you doin' tonight?" he said, as Michelle broke away from me and returned to her family of nomads who loved her.

To keep busy and not dwell on what I didn't have, I upped my travel writing byline and traveled extensively. By then, I had a monthly column in several national newspapers writing about travel shopping. My friends wanted to carry my luggage, so to speak, but I usually traveled alone.

Although I was paid very little for these columns, it was first class all the way in the finest hotels, private guides and VIP dining. All I did was pay for the roundtrip cab to and from a New York airport; the rest was expense-free. And, of course, I visited my children and family members in Rhode Island where all was going well.

On one visit, I confronted my daughter about her mother living in New York. "Tell me the truth, Lesley. Did I do the right thing leaving you with your father and brothers a few years ago? After all, I missed your first kiss; I missed buying the prom dresses. And I'm missing the day to day. Now your baby brother is gone because of me. Deep down do you hate me?"

"Mommy," she said. She rarely called me *Mommy.* "You haven't missed very much. I've accepted my life. Dad is Mr. Mom. He does a good job. I wouldn't know what to do if you came back. I like you in New York. It makes my life different. We see each other a lot. You open up your home and your floor for my friends to sleep on so we can enjoy the city. Of course you did the right thing by moving away. And you're doing the right thing for Derek, too."

"Are you sure?"

"Yes. Do something with your life, Mom, because I will."

Her validation was all I needed to continue on my life's journey, as the season changed again in my Hell's Kitchen neighborhood, also Michelle's.

<m>

New York is a city of walkers and many continued the activity when bitter winds turned the streets into bone-chilling funnels. The homeless became rounded in appearance as they layered misfit clothing to ward off freezing to death.

Some sat along the sidewalks over the warm subway exhaust grates. Many rode the subways all night.

When January 1991 arrived, I hadn't seen Michelle for a long time. But I thought about her often. In an odd way, we were friends, going on two years. So I was thrilled to almost trip over her one drizzly night as I rounded the corner of Eighth Avenue and West 58th Street. She was seated on the ground, as usual, with her legs stretched out on the sidewalk. Eugene and Philip were on either side. She was sober, clear-eyed, wore new sneakers and a reasonably clean coat. Her hair was shiny and combed under a knitted hat.

"Mrs. Browning," I said and tapped her foot with the tip of my umbrella. "It's been months. Where have you been?"

"Steve's dead," she said. Her bottom lip quivered.

I stooped to her level and touched her arm. I believed her this time. "What happened?"

"He suffered a seizure on the street. I was at Bellevue recovering from a beating when an ambulance took him to St. Clare's Hospital. He died without me. He was only 35. His family took him home to Kentucky. When I called his grandmother, she said he looked peaceful and childlike in his burial suit."

I looked at Eugene and Philip for reassurance. They nodded and lowered their head in a gesture of sadness.

"Steve sensed he was dying. He gave me this cross," Michelle said as she pulled a black shoelace from around her neck with the cross on it. "He said to keep this and go home to my family."

"What about going home, Michelle?" I asked, feeling hope she'd reunite with her family.

"My mother's coming to get me at the end of January. Eddie wrote and told her Steve died, and I'm sick. You won't believe the family I have in Italy."

Eddie Benson's name with a West 50's address was the signature on the Bellevue Hospital form that released Michelle into his care. She'd mentioned him before, adding she paid him to freshen up at his apartment.

"I'm staying at Eddie's now," she said. "And I'm never going to drink again. I've been sober for six weeks. I miss Steve so much. I want to live, Judith."

"I want you to live, too. Give me Eddie's exact address," I said and fumbled in my purse for a pen and paper.

While we spoke, Philip put his head on Michelle's lap. He asked me to call him a stretch limo so he could stretch out in it. Since I'd grown accustomed to their health complaints and my legs were cramped from stooping, I ignored him and stood up to leave.

"If you stay sober, I'll invite you and your mother to dinner at my apartment. Would you like that, Michelle?" I assumed her mother would be horrified by her daughter's appearance. She'd want to know Michelle had a friend in New York.

"I'd like that. Thank you."

"Stay sober. I'll see you soon," I said, as I left her.

Walking the few blocks to my home, I felt buoyed with the news about her mother. But how could I get Michelle into my apartment building unnoticed if she arrived drunk and smelly? New Yorkers were very particular about their privacy. But she didn't know where I lived. If I gave her my address, would she or the other homeless follow me home?

Would they accost me in the vestibule? If I gave her my telephone number, would she torment me? My questions told me I wasn't prepared to help this troubled woman on her level, only with a street friendship that suited me. The duplicity of my compassion troubled me.

But when I thought about it, Michelle never asked where I lived. She didn't ask for my phone number, where I worked or knew my last name. She accepted me fully. She allowed me to delve into her life and ask personal questions. I was only prepared to help on her street level. Taking her home wasn't on my agenda. Would I have to scrub myself and the tub with anti-lice shampoo? A shower and hot meal for several nights and then telling her to return to the streets seemed a Band-Aid solution. Although something was happening beyond our street contact, Michelle would have to earn the right to come to my home.

destined to meet

SHORTLY AFTER I LEARNED ABOUT STEVE'S death, I was on my couch watching TV, snug under a fluffy blanket. Since it was winter, I envisioned Michelle huddled under a cardboard box on the street. She told me she'd awake covered with a blanket of snow. The alcohol in her body kept her warm. I'd known Michelle for two years so it was normal for thoughts about her to float in my mind. This night, I wondered if her mother was coming. If yes, I had to keep my dinner invite.

Around 10:00 p.m., Michelle's whereabouts consumed me until I left the couch, opened a desk drawer and pulled out Eddie Benson's address. Maybe she was there. If not, I'd buy soup and go to the bank lobby or nearby subway station, hoping to find her. Without any thought for my well-being, I dressed warmly and went out into the freezing night.

As I walked alongside Roosevelt Hospital to Eddie's place, squatters sat near hot-air exhaust vents and under scaffolding. Recliner chairs and sleeping cots were shoved against a hospital wall. Blaring TV sets were plugged into pirated electrical outlets.

"Steve and I lived beside the hospital," Michelle once told me. "But we left when the crackheads moved in."

The opposite side of the street had brownstones with sagging front doors. At Eddie's address, a single lightbulb hung in the lobby hallway. I questioned my sanity when I climbed his apartment house steps and entered the vestibule. There was a slight odor of urine in the enclosed area. Names were penned on the wall beside apartment numbers listed on the intercom. I rang Eddie's bell.

"Yeah?" said a man's voice.

"Hi, I'm looking for Michelle Browning."

"Wait a minute," the voice responded.

Fear shot through my veins like hot scalding water. As I waited, I noticed a hunched woman climbing the outside stairs. She wore a black knitted hat that touched her eyeglasses. Her coat, once beige, was filthy and fastened with a large safety pin. When she entered the vestibule, I recognized Michelle.

"Oh my God, Michelle, it's you."

"Hey, what you doing here?"

"I've come to find you. How are you?"

She lowered her head. "I've been drinking. I miss Steve."

The inside door behind me opened. I jumped. Michelle looked at the small, white, frail man dressed in black who was looking suspiciously at me.

"Everything's OK, Eddie. Judith's a friend of mine," Michelle said.

"I know her from the neighborhood. I'm trying to help," I said.

And I knew him as the man I'd seen in the bank lobby one night with Steve, Michelle, Eugene and Philip. He was dressed in black, holding a portable cassette player, which he swung wildly and everyone danced.

"I'm trying to help, too," he said to me. One lone tooth jutted up from behind his pencil-thin bottom lip. It resembled a kernel of yellow corn. "Marie stays with me sometimes. I've known her and Steve, God rest his soul, for five years. You OK, baby? Looks like you've been drinking. You know, honey, you shouldn't do that."

"Go fuck yourself," she scowled.

"She doesn't mean that, Judith. Would you like to come up?" he asked softly. "What do you think, Marie?"

With her nodded approval, I followed them up five flights of stairs regardless of my lingering fear. Their trailing body odor was enough to make me cover my nose. Oddly, each flight took me back to when I was the only child of my divorced mother who moved constantly. Climbing apartment house stairs was embedded in my DNA.

My mother, Angela Glynn, stood five-feet, two-inches tall. She was gutsy, smart, good-looking and quick-witted. Soon into her marriage to my father, he drank heavily, going from job to job and stumbling up a tenement's back stairs while I grew in her womb. Mother divorced him when I was five. Without child support, she worked full time, moving from tenement to tenement on Providence's East Side.

THE STREET OR ME

<:m:>

"Excuse the mess," Eddie said, motioning for me to sit down at the kitchen table when we entered his apartment. I was horrified at its derelict condition.

He talked incessantly but the kitchen was so incredibly filthy I didn't comprehend his words. The walls were grease-yellow. The stove's once-white surface had long, finger-like streaks of blackened grease covering its sides. The aluminum pots were black. The blue squares on the linoleum's pattern were only visible at the outer edges. Years of grime had built up over the rest of the floor. A dirt-covered, worn-out path led to a closed and crackled door. I assumed that led to the rest of the floor-through apartment, which ran front to back in a straight line.

In one corner was a large plastic dishpan with hundreds of cat droppings piled ski-slope-style in the kitty litter. No cat could have piled its feces that way, I thought. Eddie did it. Beside the cat's dishpan toilet were a dozen tin cans filled with minute scraps of paper. Michelle later told me Eddie sat for hours cutting newspapers and trash into tiny pieces.

Michelle took a swig from a pint she had in her coat pocket and sat across from me. "You're bringing whores to this hellhole and stealing my money," she accused Eddie.

He gave me a sheepish look, arched his eyebrows and laughed, saying that was not true. He revealed he first befriended Michelle and Steve after seeing them around Columbus Circle. Steve was the rich boy who never worked hard for his money. Marie came from a well-to-do Italian family. She couldn't care for herself. He never saw two people more devoted to each other and he prayed for years God would help them get better.

Michelle, looking forlorn, shook her head in agreement.

Despite rosary beads hanging from a bare nail over the kitchen table filled with comic books, I didn't trust Eddie. "How long have you lived in this apartment?" I asked.

"Forty-nine years."

"Tell her how much rent you pay," Michelle chimed in.

"You're going to be jealous, Judith. I'm a rent-controlled tenant and pay $74 a month."

That was around my monthly telephone bill. "What do you do for a living?" I asked, assuming he was on welfare.

"I'm trying to get work in the theatre. Do you like Elvis Presley?" he asked and switched on a tape recorder. "You Ain't Nothin' But A Hound Dog" blared from a scratchy cassette. Eddie frantically strummed a phantom guitar. His eyes closed, his head tipped backward and his legs flapped, resembling a puppet on a string. I expected him to howl.

I guessed his age at early-sixties. He was slight in stature, a withered man with a large head and sunken cheeks. He resembled Edvard Munch's "The Scream." Eddie's long hair was dyed jet-black and tucked behind each ear, which accented his ghoulish-white complexion. He wore a stained, black wool shirt over a white turtleneck. His black wool pants ballooned at the hips. A black belt was fastened at its last hole to accentuate his narrow waist. The pants were mottled with white stains.

Michelle clapped her hands while seated on her rickety chair before jumping up to join Eddie's dance. She grabbed my hands and jerked me upright. "Come on, Judith," she slurred. "Let's jitterbug."

I was appalled. When she lifted her arm for me to pass under, her stench traveled to my stomach. I wanted to be a teenager again, sitting out the high-school dance, always the wallflower in the room. I was the pretty girl many parents told their children to avoid because my parents had divorced. I preferred that shame to the disgust of dancing missteps with Michelle.

Several times she'd sway and stop to accuse Eddie of stealing from her. He finally gave up the Elvis impersonation and sat down. Michelle stopped dancing, too. She then pushed her soiled jeans down her slender legs and pulled out a wad of money from her knee sock.

"Here," she said and counted out six one-hundred-dollar bills that she stuffed into my hand. "You keep these. I trust you. This motherfucker steals from me when I pass out. I pay him $250 a month to stay in this shit-hole and buy his food."

The unfolding event terrified me. Would Eddie attack me to get the money? Maybe there was someone dangerous behind that crackled kitchen door. Eddie looked at my eyes, at the cash in my hand, and back to Michelle, who was pulling up her soiled jeans.

"Marie, baby. There are places here to hide your money. Why would I take it?"

She couldn't focus and sat down. Her empty pint of peppermint schnapps had taken control. As I put on my coat, she asked me to wait. She got up quickly and disappeared behind the closed kitchen door. I sat alone with Eddie who looked at my hand holding Michelle's money.

"She says the strangest things, Judith. I don't steal from Marie. I love her. She's like a child to me."

"Don't worry, Eddie, I'll leave the money here. I want her to calm down."

The crackled door flung open. Michelle rushed into the kitchen clutching a tattered manila envelope. With one swift movement of her arm, she cleared the clutter from the table. It fluttered to the floor. "This is my family in Italy," she said and dumped a heap of photos on the table.

Images of her three sisters, two brothers, a robust Italian mother and a subdued father spread before me. There was a large photo of Michelle in her First Communion dress. Rosary beads draped her folded hands.

In another photo, she sat seductively in tall grass, a ravishingly beautiful young woman with flowing blond hair.

"That's me before I came to America. I won the Miss San Daniele contest," she said. Michelle's persona changed as she viewed the photos. She was gentle. Her family made her beam. "I told you about my beautiful family. You didn't believe me."

"I believed you."

"I wrote to her mother when Steve died, asking for someone to take Marie home. She's very sick and wants to die," Eddie said, interrupting Michelle's gaiety.

So Michelle was right when she said her mother was coming to New York. I learned that night Michelle also used Eddie's address to receive mail from her family. He

Mireille Turoldo, age 12 in Italy, wearing her First Communion dress.

didn't have a telephone. However, most of her mail was a stack of unpaid hospital bills on top of his refrigerator.

"When was the last time you were home?" I asked Michelle.

"Four years ago. My father died a year ago."

"Do you call your Mom regularly?"

"I call collect from a payphone. I tell her everything is fine. I'm ashamed of my true life. In Italy, they'd never understand the homeless problem. All my sisters live in beautiful homes. We had a great childhood full of life's finer things."

As her photos shuffled through our hands, I knew her mother should know about Michelle's dire straits. I was a mother, too, and would want to know. I asked for her mother's address. Maybe Michelle would let me write or call her. And when was she coming to New York to take her daughter home?

They both ignored that question about Michelle going home, but Eddie did give me soiled paper and a grimy pencil to write her mother's address. Michelle didn't comment. The $600 that was balled in my hand was now on the table. He glanced at it often.

"Michelle, it's too cold outside. Sleep here tonight," I said, as I prepared to leave.

"I will if he doesn't bring whores in."

"Judith, wait," Eddie said, ignoring her. "I want to show you something." He disappeared behind the crackled door.

Michelle and I were alone for the first time in his apartment. We spoke softly, like confidants and schoolgirls.

"He's really the Devil, you know," she whispered loudly. "He's fucking crazy, too."

"Do you pay him to stay here?"

"Yes."

"And the whores?"

She said Eddie used her money and that of another homeless woman to bring whores to his apartment. He

①

DEAR MAMA TUROLDO,

~ THIS IS MARIE + STEAVE'S
FRIEND,   WRITING TO YOU
FOR THE FIRST TIME; AND FOR A VERY
IMPORTANT REASON !!! ~

~ AS YOU KNOW, STEAVE WOULD
NOT GO HOME TO HIS FAMILY, BECAUSE
HE DID NOT WANT TO LEAVE MARIE !!!
... AND MARIE WOULD NOT COME HOME
TO HER FAMILY BECAUSE, SHE WOULD
NOT LEAVE STEVE !!! ~

~ NOW, SHE WANT'S TO COME
HOME TO HER MAMA, BROTHER'S AND
SISTER'S; BECAUSE, SHE HAS
NOTHING TO HOLD HER, HERE ANY MORE
YOU SEE, ON NOV. 10TH, 1990, ...
HER HUSBAND, STEVE, DIED IN THE
HOSPITAL OF A STROKE !!! HE WAS
ONLY 35 YEAR'S OLD !!! ~

~ OVER: ↗

②

~ MARIE IS HEART-BROKEN AND
WANT'S TO DIE, ALSO! BUT, SHE
STILL LOVE'S HER BEAUTIFUL
FAMILY; AND SHE WANTS TO BE
WITH YOU, AGAIN!!! ~

~ SHE IS VERY SICK, JUST
LIKE STEVE AND SHE NEED'S YOU
AND YOUR LOVE AND UNDERSTANDING.
PLEASE, I BEG YOU, IF YOU STILL
LOVE LITTLE MARIE, ... PLEASE, PLEASE
SEND SOMEONE TO GET HER AND TAKE
HER HOME TO HER FAMILY AND LOVED-
ONE'S ... WHILE THERE'S STILL A
CHANCE!!! ~ I WILL WATCH OVER
HER AND PROTECT HER UNTIL YOU
CAN COME FOR HER!!! ~ I DO THIS
IN JESUS NAME!!! ~

~ BUON NATALI,

wouldn't let men in, although Steve could stay on occasion since he and the other homeless men pooled their money so Michelle could stay overnight. I couldn't fault Eddie completely. He gave her a bed. She ate a hot meal. She washed in his filthy bathroom. I couldn't take her home. I was terrified of body lice and the unpredictable behavior of alcoholics, so I left her on the street.

The paint-chipped door opened swiftly. Eddie leapt into the kitchen. "Ta dah," he sang and landed on one foot.

"Jesus Christ," I blurted out.

A grotesque, full-size, rubber Batman mask covered his head. One arm swung in an arched motion carrying with it one side of a full-length, black, velvet cape. He wrapped it across his chest and paraded around the kitchen. The cape swirled from side to side.

"I told you he's nuts," Michelle said, doubling in laughter.

"How do you like this, Judith?" Eddie's voice was muffled behind the mask. His piercing black eyes had a wild, glazed look coming from the slits.

"You're quite a guy. You can go from Elvis to Batman in one night."

Michelle giggled. "He wears that costume on the street. He even wore it to visit Steve in the hospital."

"I've got to go home," I said. I was numb. But Michelle's $600 was still on the table. I looked at it, as did Eddie through his Batman mask. Michelle reached for it.

"Here, take it, take it," she insisted and put the wad in my hand.

"Marie, we have places here to put it," Eddie said.

I left the money on the table and approached the apartment door as a knee-bending relief engulfed me. A few hours earlier, I'd been curled under my mohair blanket, staring at TV, and now I was in this bizarre hellhole of a walk-up with a drunken homeless woman pulling $600 from her sock and a toothless Elvis-Batman freak.

Michelle got up from her chair but fell to the floor. I rushed to her side. Her arms wrapped around me as I picked her up.

"I love you, Judith," she whispered and placed her head in my neck. "It's not a coincidence we met. There's a reason."

And like the protector I'd unwittingly become from the moment I first saw Michelle, I held her close, no longer fearful, at least not that night, of the diseases or body lice she might carry.

"I love you, too, hon. Get a good night's sleep. We'll talk soon."

I ran down the five flights and out into the darkness. Within ten minutes, I was on my living-room couch staring out the window at luminous skyscrapers, reeling from what had happened in Eddie's apartment. It overwhelmed me to think Michelle tried for years to recreate a taste of home in that incredible filth.

For the two years I'd known her, my life was normal except for financial issues. I'd moved to a slightly larger apartment. Between freelance projects, travel articles, steady temp secretary jobs and terrific women friends, my life in New York was happy. But Michelle was still the drunken homeless woman in my neighborhood. People asked if I bothered with her because my father was an alcoholic whom I'd seen lying in the streets of downtown Providence. Was I righting his wrong? Did I want to write an article about the homeless? Michelle was perfect fodder.

I couldn't answer since I'd asked myself the same questions when I'd walk away from Michelle, season after season. Caring deeply made no sense. Now, this night I'd put myself in danger by entering into an apartment occupied by a crazy man. But with Michelle's hug and whispered *it's not a coincidence we met*, my days of walking away from her were over. But did I have the right to control her life? And how would I do it? What could I do beyond what I'd already done?

As I lay in my warm and comfortable bed and Michelle was in Eddie's hellish apartment, I vowed to increase my impact on her life. I'd up the value of my gifts and street friendship. I'd instill her with unconditional hope. Hers was gone. But she'd find it again when I got under her skin as deeply as she was under mine. Somehow, I'd get her to choose me over her street life.

chasing the jackpot

A WEEK LATER, I PASSED THE CHASE ATM lobby, and looked through its plate-glass window. Since it was evening, bright lights illuminated the space. Eugene stood in a corner. Philip sat on a window ledge. That night a soiled mattress had been pulled into the large open area. Three people lay on it. I couldn't see Michelle's face so I looked for the grubby red boots she wore for weeks on end. Sometimes the homeless person's feet were their only identifiable body part when they huddled together. Hers were on the mattress.

Thinking she'd be hungry, I left the window and crossed the street to purchase soup for her at the nearby restaurant. When I returned to the bank, Philip recognized me and rushed to open the door. His sweeping arm welcomed me in. By now, we were friends. His eyes would fix on mine and not on the ground or wander into the distance when we spoke. He was always included in my conversations with Michelle. They were a couple after Steve died.

"You're different from the others who try to help," he'd observed, as we grew to know each another better.

How different, I wondered, and in what way? For sure, I had no social work training. I had no book knowledge or hands-on experience with severely addicted people. I had no one to call for advice since most of my family and friends thought it odd I reached out to Michelle and her derelict companions. Even the medical community I encountered with her in hospitals viewed me with skepticism. I had limited financial resources to buy my way into her life. I wouldn't take her to my home. Plus, I continually put myself in danger, especially late at night, when I looked for her. There was no one to give me a raise at work for a charitable job well done. She wasn't part of a corporation's Community Outreach program. I wasn't looking for fame or approval. My quest was somewhat hidden from public view. I was alone as anyone could be reaching out to Michelle.

So what did I have with her, and reluctant Philip, to convince them I was the real deal? Longevity knowing them was one asset. I'd developed a deep and unconditional love for Michelle during our years together, and she knew it. I grieved deeply for her plight. I discovered an untapped compassion for women who sank so low. I had a quick wit and used it, not as a put-down, but to counterbalance the horror she and her gang experienced daily. I could tell fabulous, lively stories, which Michelle loved. I had humility, fear, conviction, sobriety and the dignity of a woman who had changed her life to survive. I wanted Michelle to emulate me, pompous as that seemed. I was also a writer and innately knew the beginning, middle and end of a story.

What I didn't know was I shared poor health with Michelle. I'd learn years later that as I tried to return her to her family, to a dignified womanhood and to sobriety, I carried the deadly hepatitis C virus in my blood. It had been asymptomatically replicating daily in my liver from the late-1970s when I received a transfusion during a hysterectomy.

"Michelle, wake up," I said and shook her shoulder. "It's Judith. I've got hot soup filled with meat and potatoes."

Her eyes blinked open, slowly. She tried to raise herself using one arm but fell back down with a thud. Her eyes couldn't focus. Her body odor was horrific. Her distended stomach resembled a pregnancy. Her hair was matted with grime. Her face was swollen. Several runny sores were at the corners of her mouth. Mumbling my name, she asked how I was doing.

"She's real sick this time," Philip said as he lifted his arm. "Damn," he said, as his hand went inside his jacket and he scratched. "These bugs are biting something awful." He then withdrew his hand and placed body lice on one thumbnail. With the other thumb, he flattened the bugs. Someone who worked with the homeless told me some homeless people remain smelly and infested with body lice as a maneuver to keep people away.

"Michelle, we have to get you sober before your mother arrives," I said.

"My mother's here?" she said and struggled to get up.

"No, not yet. When is she coming?"

"The end of January."

"It's the end of January now."

"It is?"

"You have to go to the hospital tonight and get better before she gets here," I said and pulled her upright. She was heavy and incredibly drunk. "Philip," I shouted over to him, "she's going with me to Roosevelt."

"OK, Judy," he said, but he was more engrossed with his body lice than interacting with me. "Marie, I'll visit you tomorrow in the hospital."

Several people came to the bank's entrance, looked in at the homeless sprawled on the mattress, Michelle trying to get up and at Philip picking and squashing lice. They stared at me. Maybe I was with The Salvation Army. No one came inside to help or to use the ATM machines; instead, they turned away.

Michelle and I stumbled over to the door. I tried to hold it open and pass through with her. We were hit with a blast of freezing wind. She didn't flinch, but I pulled my hat over my ears and buttoned the top of my coat. Another blast of wind hit us, as the opened door created a funnel effect that pushed me back inside the bank.

"I'll go, too," Eugene said. He'd been watching us from the sidelines.

He was a dear man and deeply concerned about Michelle's health. Many times, he'd take me aside and whisper softly, repeating the same sentences about her need to go home. He couldn't look anyone straight in the eye and stared to the side or down when he spoke. He told me repeatedly that his parents were deceased.

When we reached the street, Eugene took one of Michelle's elbows into his strong hand. I placed my arm in her other elbow and clenched it to my body. She leaned in half with a bug-eyed expression. Her head was cocked to the same side as the shoulder that led her. Her strength was astounding.

"Hey, hold it, Marie," Eugene said, responding to her force that pulled us along. "She got to stop drinking. She ain't gonna make it," he said to me. "Every time she talks about Steve, she drinks."

"Is her mother coming for her?" I asked, as steam evaporated from my breath.

"Dunno. Marie says she's coming."

The emergency room at Roosevelt was right off the Ninth Avenue entrance. But to get to it, Michelle had to climb several stairs, which wasn't an easy task. I pulled her by the elbow and Eugene pushed from behind. When we entered, ten people were waiting to be seen. All eyes stared at us. A sign directed new patients to the Triage Nurse.

"I'm embarrassed. I smell," Michelle mumbled, as we approached the Triage Nurse station.

"This is Michelle Browning. She needs help," I said to the admitting nurse.

"We know her well. What's wrong tonight, Michelle?" she asked, appearing to hold her breath as Michelle's odor floated her way.

"I have hepatitis, ulcers, high blood pressure, a heart problem, and I'm an alcoholic," she said, listing her health problems as attributes.

"Can you admit her?" I asked.

"Not for alcoholism," the nurse replied and looked at me as if I should have known.

Michelle would have to return the next morning at 9:00 a.m. and voluntarily admit herself into the detox program, returning daily. I was shocked. Here was a woman obviously drunk and in need of medical care.

"We can admit her for alcohol-related problems only, not drunkenness," the nurse told me when I asked again if Michelle could be admitted that night.

After taking Michelle's blood pressure and temperature, the nurse told us to sit in the waiting room, which we did. She didn't say for how long. I didn't dare ask. Michelle's odor cleared out our section, as several patients moved to the farthest point away. One person offered Michelle a bottle of perfume. She splashed herself with the fragrance, as did I.

"Motherfuckers," Michelle mumbled and spat blood on the floor. "I'm dying and they won't let me in this hospital."

"Shut up and wait your turn. You have to get better before your mother gets here," I scolded.

"How can I face her? Look at how I look. My mother will yell at me." She wept openly.

"Don't cry here. We have to be quiet. Sober up some day and I guarantee you'll look better."

"Will you send me home in a body bag if I die on the street?"

"Yes, but I'd rather send you home sober."

The hours stretched on. Realizing I had to check my home recorder and needed change for the payphone, I asked Michelle for a quarter.

"You want money from me? Now that's a switch," she said and handed me change just as the hospital's plate-glass door opened.

Eddie Benson walked in with a flourish. He wore all black. How did he know we were there? Maybe he'd gone to the bank lobby looking for Michelle. He sashayed in front of us, then stopped to hover over Michelle.

"Marie, baby. What are you doing here tonight?"

"I'm sick. Judith brought me here."

"Come home with Eddie. I have a bed for you. But you got to be quiet going up the stairs. My neighbors complain to the management company about you. What do you think, Judith?"

"She's staying with me."

"Marie's been drinking heavily since Steve died. I don't know what to do anymore," he said.

When Eddie mentioned Steve, Michelle wailed. He said many people tried to help them. Not only me, but there was Dr. Conrad Fischer from the hospital. Eddie asked her again if she wanted to go home with him.

"Go fuck yourself. I'm staying with Judith."

And as quickly as Eddie entered the hospital's waiting room, he vanished into the night.

"He's the Devil, you know," she said to me.

"I think you're right."

"God's going to take care of you, honey, for what you're trying to do for this lady," said a woman seated across from Michelle and me. Her wise, grandmotherly black face was framed with a turban. She wore a housecoat and slippers. She said she had cancer and was diabetic. Since the hospital was full, her emergency room wait had stretched into 24 hours.

I didn't know about God helping me, I only wanted to help Michelle recuperate in time for her mother's visit. However, when this woman spoke to us, I had an idea. The more people who supported my quest for Michelle to go home, the more she might make it a reality.

"If you were a mother, what would you do if Michelle was your daughter?" I asked the woman, now part of our story.

"You got to clean up your act, honey, and stop drinking. Your mother loves you no matter what," the woman said.

"I'm going to get a beer," Michelle said and stood up, ignoring the woman's advice.

"Sit down. Don't you dare walk out on me," I demanded.

She obeyed. I opened my pocketbook and gave Michelle a recent photograph of myself, one I'd been meaning to give to her. On its back, I wrote my full name, address and telephone number. "When you fill out a form and it asks for a next of kin, put down my information. I'll take care of you."

"I'll never lose this," she said and held my photo next to her heart. She then bent over and removed one filthy red boot. Her hand struggled downward into an elasticized sock and pulled out a crumpled bulge. She counted out two, moist, one-hundred dollar bills and told me to keep them. If she were admitted to the hospital, the staff would steal her money.

The people around us stared in disbelief. I had no choice but to take the money, which I put in an empty cigarette box I found nearby and then into my purse. Now I was Michelle's treasurer, a secondary position to her being Philip's.

By 2:00 a.m., Michelle's body craved alcohol that was beyond her control. "I'm getting the fuck out of here," she said and ran to the door. She pushed it open, ran down the stairway and onto the sidewalk.

I was furious. Four hours wasted in an emergency room with a homeless, smelly drunk. I left the waiting room, ran down the stairs and caught up with her mid-block. "Slow down, Michelle. Walk with me. I'm afraid to be alone at this hour," I said.

"I'm going back to the bank lobby. Philip and Eugene will be waiting for me. Hold that money. Everyone thinks I'm crazy, but I'm just drunk," were her parting words.

When I arrived home, I put the cigarette box with the moist dollar bills in my desk drawer. What a joke. She had $200 in her sock and I was behind on my mortgage. She had free health care and I had none. Now what? Would Michelle and her cronies call me at all hours since I held their stash? What had I done to myself?

I didn't want to believe it but I knew Michelle didn't want anyone's help. She'd have to help herself before I'd compromise myself again. I wasn't cut out for our escalating relationship. I had my own fish to fry, financial problems to resolve and my children needed me. I was all alone out there on some Godforsaken mission I couldn't understand. But maybe I would understand her problem if I knew why she couldn't stop her addiction in the face of a horrendous street-life existence.

Dr. Fischer's name came to mind. I rolled over in bed, called Roosevelt Hospital and had him paged, ignoring the late hour.

"Dr. Fischer?" I asked hesitantly when a man answered.

"You got him," said a strong, upbeat voice.

A long explanation of my involvement with Michelle followed. I asked about her medical condition. I asked about Steve and her inability to stop drinking.

"I know Michelle but haven't seen her recently. I treated Steve over the years. His parents wanted him home. Michelle is to blame for his death. She wouldn't let him go."

I gasped.

Dr. Fischer recalled one incident when Steve was admitted to the hospital with a full-blown case of the DTs. He shook uncontrollably and saw things on the wall. After a successful treatment, the doctor arranged for Steve to enter a New York halfway house for alcoholics. Steve agreed and was released. That same day Dr. Fischer saw Steve, Michelle and other homeless people drinking in a doorway. He was angry with her because she'd stopped Steve from going to the halfway house. He admired me for trying to get her home. That gave him hope. But he thought she had one chance in infinity to get off the streets. She loved her addiction, and she loved street life.

"I don't know how I got in this deep. But I've talked to her for a few years and keep getting in deeper," I said.

"Don't ever let her in your home. She doesn't have a conscience. She'll steal you blind."

"I was in the emergency room with her tonight. Why was she shaking when she ran out to get a beer?"

"When alcohol wears off, people as addicted as Michelle have to replace the craving with more alcohol or, in severe cases, admission to the hospital and medical treatment. That's Michelle," he said lightheartedly. "We know her well. She's been admitted countless times. As soon as she feels better, she walks out. By now, I suspect she's too far gone. Death will occur in less than a year. What about her family in Italy?"

"Her mother is supposed to be here by now. If I write to her and explain the desperate situation her daughter is in, maybe that will speed things up. Can you help me?"

"Sure, but Michelle will manipulate you until the end. Put a bag over her head to get her out of the country. Keep me posted."

As I lay in bed, I thought about the alcoholics I'd booted from my life. Lots of people drink. But alcoholics are talented liars who manipulate until caught. Life with a lying, belligerent, masochistic, self-absorbed alcoholic would always be horrendous. And I understood why my mother preferred the pain of divorcing my alcoholic father to being an enabler. A friend said all alcoholics hit the "jackpot" before recovery begins. A car crash, job loss or something life-changing needs to overpower the addiction.

After talking with Dr. Fischer, I envisioned Michelle asleep on a soiled mattress, curled next to Philip. Why would I dump other alcoholics in my life yet stay in hers? She chased her jackpot daily. It was all a mystery to me.

the street or me

MY NEW YORK LIFE WASN'T ALL ABOUT Michelle. After four years of writing my travel shopping newspaper column, I couldn't continue even with the free travel and paid expenses. I'd lost interest in travel; all airports looked the same, plus a new city map bored me. I couldn't find the creative juice to capture the flavor of a destination, which indicated it was time to put my travel notes away and concentrate on finding lucrative full-time work since temp secretarial assignments were drying up due to a lackluster economy.

The irony of trying to improve the quality of Michelle's life was the awful financial state I was in. Mortgaged to the hilt; a college loan for Derek; high credit card charges; no life or health insurance and my love life stunk. A return to Rhode Island wasn't doable. It was worse there. But New York still exhilarated me. After five years, it was home, so I decided to splurge with a birthday party to honor my New York friends and my Rhode Island family. Cleaning Michelle up and asking her to attend passed my mind but her presence would upset people. It would be a ladies-only party, except for my three sons. Michelle would have to care for herself while I planned my special day.

But Michelle was incapable of taking control of her life, evidenced one night when I passed an apartment building vestibule on Eight Avenue. Philip saw me and rushed to open the door. Eugene was also inside and drinking from a paper bag. Michelle yanked it from him but started to cry when she saw me. "I want to die," she said and wiped her runny nose against her sleeve.

"She threw herself in front of a cab tonight. I saved her," Eugene said, revealing a sense of pride for what he'd done.

"Don't die on me now, Michelle. It's the booze and this hellish life that makes you suicidal," I said.

"I can't stand it anymore. I miss Steve. I want to die," she said between sobs.

"Nothing will bring him back. Honor him with your sobriety. What about going home? Your mother didn't come. It's mid-February. Maybe she was never coming. Do you want to die in front of a cab or at home with your family?"

"It's impossible to go on," she screamed.

This time, there was something different about her anguish. She was deadly serious and suicidal. Her days were numbered, either by her own hand or by alcoholism. I believed the only person to keep her alive would be her mother.

"Let me write to your mother. I beg you. What about Italy and going home, Michelle? We both know your mother isn't coming to America to get you. Maybe she doesn't know you're this bad. Maybe Eddie's letter didn't have an impact. You must know that dignity should be part of everyone's life and in death too. Do you want to die in front of a cab or at home with your family? There's still hope. You can live a better life far from the streets of New York."

"No. No. What will she think of me?"

"I won't write unless you say yes. I'm begging you, Michelle. You have to make a choice here. It's street life or me."

"No, no, no, no," she sobbed and backed into a corner of the cramped vestibule. She repeated the same fears about what her mother would think. The humiliation was deep.

I turned to Philip for help. "Talk to her. I can't write to her mother without permission. Michelle said she was coming but that's not true."

"You gotta let Judy write to your mother. This is no life for you. Baby, you gotta go home soon. Things change," he said.

"I can't face them," she wailed and slid to the floor where she buried her face in her bent knees.

Philip reassured Michelle her mother loved her. She'd accept her. He was caring, eloquent and convincing.

"Let Judy write to your mother. You gotta go home Marie," Eugene added.

It seemed like hours but I'm sure only a few minutes passed until Michelle lifted her head. Despair was in her eyes when they met mine. "Yes, you can write to her," she finally said.

"I'll write the letter tonight and send it by FedEx tomorrow. We'll have an answer soon. Hold on a little longer."

The building's maintenance man entered the vestibule and stopped in his tracks when he saw us. We were ordered to leave as he shoved Eugene onto the sidewalk. Michelle, Philip and I followed voluntarily.

"Listen closely. This is a defining moment for us. Don't kill yourself," I said, looking deep into Michelle's bloodshot eyes, now filled with deep suffering. I put my hands on her shoulders. "Hold on. I love you, Michelle."

As I walked away, the look on her face was one of incredible agony. I knew she wanted me to take her into my arms and into my home that night. She was too ashamed to ask. The pain I felt was unbearable. How could I deny her this night above all others? But I couldn't give in and take her home. Every part of my being said no. As I began to walk away, a deep groan came out of her.

"Judith," she wailed on the busy sidewalk where we'd talked often, "no matter what happens to me, I want you to know I love you. But I don't know if I can make it through the night."

Although countless people rushed by us on Eighth Avenue and some stopped to watch, confused by the spectacle, I felt incredibly alone out there. "Hang on a little longer. Your hell is almost over," I said, but I didn't approach her. "Take care of her, Philip," I said to him, as I turned my back on her and walked home.

My lips quivered and tears moistened my cheeks as I rounded the corner to my apartment building. There was pain in my heart. I wanted to vomit. But despite the emotions, one thought kept reoccurring: Michelle had to love herself more than she loved me. That would be the only way to kill her addiction. She'd have to suffer with street life a little longer. All I could give her was hope. That was my quest from the beginning. Taking her home was charity, not hope. The letter to her mother was composed before I turned on my computer.

<m>

Dear Mrs. Turoldo,

For the past two years, I have watched your daughter, Mireille, get sicker and sicker on the streets of New York. I am surprised she is still alive. I'll explain what has happened in the many years she has lived in the United States.

Mireille is one of the city's homeless people. She has no permanent home, sleeps on the ground, in subway stations, in apartment house doorways and bank lobbies. People walk by or walk over her. When Steve was alive, they both slept on the streets. Your daughter is alcoholic and cannot help herself any more. She and Steve begged for money. Now Mireille begs with two other men. On occasion, she lives with Eddie Benson but he takes her money in exchange for a dirty bed.

Tonight I saw Mireille, and she was very drunk. She has a broken nose, wears filthy clothes and she smells. She tried to kill herself by throwing herself in front of a taxi.

I know about you and her beautiful family. She showed me many family pictures. What she once was and once had are what keep her dreaming and alive. Her life here is hell. You would be shocked to see your daughter today.

Many times she's been in the hospital as a charity person but when she feels better, she walks out. Unless Mireille makes the commitment to stop drinking, there is nothing anyone can do. The doctors say her liver is badly damaged, and she has a heart murmur.

She told me you were coming to the United States at the end of January to take her home but you are still not here. Mireille said if you are afraid to come, can one of her sisters or another family member make the trip?

I will be your contact here since she has no apartment (Eddie asked her to leave). She is very afraid about what you will say when you see her. I am a mother with four children and beg you to have love and compassion for Mireille.

If she dies soon, I think she should have a loving family around her. She needs long-term psychiatric help and love from her family to recover. Mireille knows I am writing to you, so please respond soon. I can help with anything you need in New York. There is still some life left in your daughter's eyes. Please come and get her.

My best wishes to you.

❖m❖

Enclosed with the bombshell about to cross the Atlantic was a recent photograph of her desolate daughter standing outside the bank with Eugene and a photo of me I hoped her mother would see I was a decent woman, not someone trying to harm or exploit her family.

Before I entered the Federal Express office the next day, I questioned if I should disrupt the Turoldo family's life with my bombshell. Who was I to control Michelle's life? And what would happen if no one answered me? Despite

Above and opposite: Eugene and Michelle outside former Chase Bank in Columbus Circle, NYC, January 1991

my concerns, I sent the letter. As I awaited news from Italy, I'd go to the bank lobby at night to keep Michelle updated.

"Watch this, Judith," she said while panhandling. "Excuse me, sir," she said to an unsuspecting man as he put his card in the ATM, "but when you finish your electronic, financial transaction, could you spare some change?" She sat on a window ledge, legs crossed with one extended outward. Her folded hands cupped one knee. She winked at me during her performance.

The man appeared to ignore her; however, he dropped money into her outstretched cup on his way out. She winked at me again.

Michelle never inquired about her pending departure, only Philip, Eugene and the other homeless were interested. But she did wonder if her sisters would buy her new clothes. And she cried whenever she mentioned her mother. Sometimes she'd insist she wouldn't go home. I knew that was the bottle talking.

"You'd drink, too, if you lived like an animal. People don't understand what it's like to be homeless," she said once.

Michelle was angry because Philip broke the present she'd bought for her mother. It was a plastic, see-through, domed container. When turned upside down, the snow drifted down on a winter scene.

"He smashed it on me," she said. "Why you do that, Philip? You knew it was for my mother."

Photo of Judith Glynn enclosed with letter to Mrs. Turoldo, January 1991

He didn't answer, only stared at the wall. His act told me there was hostility within him. He was angry she was leaving him. At the last minute, would he convince her to stay with him? But, then again, when she said she wouldn't go home, he'd interrupt and insist it was the only way. He also said she could return to New York and to him if she wanted. He'd send money for the ticket.

"Ever notice how ugly people are?" Philip asked me while we waited for Michelle's mother to respond. "Especially people with long noses. Look at their faces. They are dumb-ass ugly, man. And thousands of rats and roaches crawling around. New York is a rotten, filthy city not fit for humans."

"It's fit to live in, Philip. Your perspective is from the ground up," I said.

"Can't trust nobody. Do you hear me, Marie? Not one soul. You gotta be careful," he added, gulping at a bottle of Thunderbird wine.

<m>

Although born and raised Irish-Catholic, I became a non-church-goer after my divorce. But I didn't question my charitable heart. I still prayed and thanked Him when it was going good and occasionally asked for help when it wasn't. But there was something about my years with Michelle and our ramped-up friendship that had spirituality to it. I felt chosen for the deed to get her home but not prepared for the emotions, fears, doubts and tactics that came with the odyssey. *Chosen* was a strong word. But I needed that crutch to understand my devotion to her.

During my lunch hours and while waiting for Mrs. Turoldo's response, I'd go to St. Patrick's Cathedral on Fifth Avenue. I prayed repeatedly for the right words and the strength to continue. That night when I saw Michelle at the bank, the right words came. I promised she could drink on the plane. I promised a round-trip ticket if she hated Italy. She could return to street life. I don't know why I said all those things because I didn't mean it, but I did.

Six days passed, the letter had been delivered and no call from the Turoldo family. Then a horrible doubt surfaced. If the family never responds, I'd handed Michelle a death sentence of lost hope. Waiting for the Turoldo family's answer was my lowest point in knowing Michelle. To counteract my angst, I began to write about our life together.

Writing was my catharsis in life. I discovered the gift in my late-thirties. The wrenching pain of a divorce that disrupted the lives of four other people because I loved my sanity and myself more healed somewhat when I put words on paper.

Writing took me to foreign lands as a freelance travel writer where I became culturally enriched. Writing taught me to be a good listener. I learned to draw people out in an interview. The rejections for articles taught me resilience. Another valuable lesson was the ability to plot out scenes. I could create the story from start to finish.

Late at night and while I awaited Mrs. Turoldo's answer, I'd sit in my apartment only a few blocks from where Michelle and I met, knowing she was probably sleeping in the bank lobby. I'd stare at the computer screen and work through a maze of emotions, then concentrate on how to handle her fears. I conceptualized how to arrange her departure, determined to box her in so tight she'd have to obey my demands. No more nice talk. I'd go to the Italian Consulate's office in New York City and ask them to prepare her travel documents. Alitalia Airlines was on my list. Dr. Fischer would be contacted. And I'd continue to go to the bank at night to win Michelle's trust and that of Philip's and Eugene's.

Despite my bravado with Michelle's life, I was growing weary and tired of homelessness. I wasn't working every day. My bills continued to pile up. How could I get involved with her family's arrival when I dreaded opening my mailbox? Plus, my birthday party was two weeks away with 25 people about to cram into my little apartment. Michelle was becoming a nuisance.

the michelle takeover

"IS THIS JUDITH GLYNN?"A MAN ASKED in halting English when I answered the phone. The ping of an international call was in the background.

"Yes. Yes, it is."

"My name is Paolo," he said. "I am calling for the mother of Mireille Turoldo. She received your letter. The family wants her home. Can you put her in the hospital so she can make the trip?"

I remembered his name as the young man who arrived at Eddie Benson's apartment looking for Michelle. I greeted him warmly, expressing my pleasure to talk to someone from Michelle's family but this was a drastic situation. The hospital won't admit her for alcoholism only. She was too sick to make the trip alone. Could he come and get her? She had to leave New York soon.

"No, no. I can't come. I'm busy with work."

"But she can go home, Paolo? That's what you're saying?"

"Yes, the family wants her home but she must call her mother first. Is she staying with you?"

I felt odd saying no since I'd written such a heartfelt letter. Paolo had to wonder why she wasn't. But it was too complicated to explain so I told him she slept on the bank floor at night. During the day, she rode the subways or walked the streets, drunk. I stressed again how sick she was.

"Yes, we know. Tell Mireille she must contact her mother. I'll call you in two days."

"I'll do my best."

"And Judith," he continued with a compassionate tone, "Her mother and the family thank you."

When I hung up, I raised my tearing eyes to the heavens. I whispered thank you. Michelle was finally going home.

My elevator couldn't take me to the street fast enough to tell her but it was too early for her to be in the bank lobby. I ran to the Columbus Circle subway entrance and down the staircase holding the shiny railing for balance. It was the same entrance where I'd first seen Michelle Browning years before. I scanned the station. She wasn't there. But Muskrat was seated on the ground singing to himself.

"Have you seen Michelle?" I said as I ran toward him.

"Nope."

"If you do, tell her to wait for me at the bank tonight."

"OK. Any news from her mother?"

"That's what it's all about, Muskrat."

"Hey, Judy, will you take me back to Ireland?"

"What do you think I am? Homeless Tours?"

Muskrat doubled with laughter as I ran up the subway stairs and returned home. At 10:00 p.m., I walked to the bank and found Michelle sitting on the window ledge. Philip and Eugene were nearby.

"Michelle, Paolo called me," I said, walking over to her.

She was relatively sober. She stared at me, sat up ramrod straight and sucked in her breath. "Paolo. Oh! What did he say? My mother received the letter?"

"Yes, she received it. Your family wants you home."

"When is my mother coming?"

"You have to call her first. Then we make plans."

She became hysterical, covering her face with her filthy hands. "What am I going to say now? You told my mother everything. She's going to yell."

"I'm a mother. She won't yell at you."

Michelle jumped off the ledge and paced. "I won't go home," she declared into the air. "I'm not going home."

"What are you talking about?" I screamed at her. "We spent hours talking about this. I wrote to your mother. Paolo called and you won't go. You selfish bitch! Sometimes I hate you, really hate you. Do you want to end up like Steve?"

Philip intervened. He appeared shocked at my outburst. He put his strong hands with their crackled skin on Michelle's shoulders. "You're dying, baby. Things cannot be the same forever. This here's no life for a woman. Listen to Judy. You gotta go home. My $1,000 comes the first of the month. You can have it."

"Michelle, we can go shopping. You'll get a haircut. You can stay with me until someone comes from Italy. Your long nightmare is almost over. Listen to Philip," I said.

"Judy, when's the first of the month?" Philip asked.

"In three days."

"You cocksuckin' motherfucker," he screamed at Eugene standing nearby. "You told me the first was tomorrow."

"Are you sure, Judy? Three days?" Philip asked.

"I'm positive."

I was also dumbfounded standing alone in the bank's ATM lobby with a group of homeless, smelly people and no one knew what day it was. I was moving mountains to get Michelle home to Italy and now she didn't want to go.

"You gotta go, Marie. I'll help you," Philip said.

"Thank you, Philip," I whispered, totally drained.

Before I left the bank, I told Michelle that Paolo would call me in two days to arrange her departure. She had to call her mother immediately.

"OK. I'll call tomorrow collect from a payphone."

But she barely made eye contact with me when I said goodbye. Instead, she retreated to a corner, slid down and became a rounded ball of a woman seated on the floor. Her expression combined meekness and terror.

The next night I stayed home. I was angry with Michelle. She'd better call her mother. I'd help with the necessary papers then it was goodbye Michelle and hello to my life on hold. But no matter how hard I tried to push Michelle away, I'd grown to love her. She was important to me. I was the last link between her life and death. What an odd, stressful and awesome destiny to behold.

Paolo called again. He asked if I'd seen Mireille.

"Yes. Did she call her mother?"

"No. But she must if she's coming home."

"She told me she saw her mother four years ago. Is that true?"

"Mireille hasn't been home in ten years. Her father died three years ago."

"Paolo, it's important I tell her what family member is coming."

"Can she come home alone?"

"No. She's too sick and confused. Someone from the family has to come here."

Paolo paused for his response. And it was then the picture became clear. How would anyone in her family cope with American paperwork, much less their half-woman, half-animal absent relative I'd presented to them? I feared no one would come for Michelle, despite their good intentions. She'd die waiting. I'd be asked to send her body home. There seemed only one solution. And it popped out of my mouth.

"Do you want me to take her home? The family has to pay for our tickets and my time because I can't lose money from not working. We have to leave soon. If I tell her that her family can't come, I guarantee she'll kill herself."

"It might be the only way," he said. "But I must consult with the family. I'll call back in an hour."

Waiting for Paolo's call, I regretted my proposal. How was I going to accomplish it? I hadn't even taken Michelle to my home. Now I'd offered to take her to Italy.

"OK, the family agrees," Paolo said with his next call. "We spoke to an important priest and a hospital was found for Mireille. The family will never leave her side. Would you like to stay with us for one week? Can you arrange to bring her medical records? And, please, she must call her mother," he said.

When we hung up, I wondered how I'd accomplish this incredible task. I said we'd fly in one week. The thought of being alone with Michelle petrified me. How could I handle the details and her need for alcohol? Even though I was now her destiny, the street was my out. Since I was an experienced traveler, the trip didn't frighten me. I'd been in and out of airports, fought jet lag and had worn out passports before their expiration. I calculated our travel time to be approximately 14 hours door to door. I had successfully created a bridge between Michelle and her family in Italy but it terrified me to cross it with her.

The next day, I was in the Italian Consulate's office on Park Avenue, meeting with a government representative. I explained Michelle's plight and reached into my purse for the recent photograph of Michelle and Eugene looking destitute and filthy. I slid it in front of the man. "Can you help me get her out of New York and home to her family in Italy?" I asked, as tears formed.

"Is she Italian?" he gasped. When he regained his composure, he asked if she had an Italian passport or birth certificate.

I confirmed she was Italian. She'd been in the States for many years, had married an American, but they ended up on the New York streets. She'd been homeless for about eight years. I'd known her for the last two. I knew she had a birth certificate because it was in the manila envelope Michelle tossed on Eddie's table the night she showed me photos of her family.

"You must bring her here with the birth certificate. I need two passport photos to issue a one-way, temporary travel document to get her out of the States," the representative said.

I told him I thought her mother was coming to get her, but it was too complicated. I offered to bring her home. Would he please call her mother and assure her I wasn't a crazy woman. Her daughter couldn't live this way. I was only helping. I was a mother, too.

"I'll call tomorrow and give you all the help you need. This is a remarkable story. Good luck, Miss Glynn."

My next stop was Alitalia Airline on Fifth Avenue. Michelle's photograph was shown to a ticketing agent. I'd chosen March 7th as our departure date, a week away.

"But what about this woman's health and sobriety?" the agent asked. "She cannot fly drunk and unruly. You will be asked to deplane."

I promised Michelle would be sober and eyed a promotional poster that offered a $100 companion fare deal.

Paolo and I spoke again. The family would meet us in Venice after Michelle and I changed planes in Milan.

"Did Michelle call her mother?" I asked. Calling her *Mireille*, her given name, was odd for me to say. I knew her as Michelle and Marie so I stuck with my protocol.

"No. But she must before we buy the tickets."

✂m✄

For my birthday party in my apartment a few days later, I'd invited my mother, in addition to my friends and children. She never visited me in New York and had disapproved of me leaving Rhode Island, so her presence was welcomed. My children were asked to bring unwanted clothing for my homeless friends. Before my party began, I took my children to meet Michelle and her homeless buddies. The clothing box overflowed.

Michelle sat on a fire hydrant that jutted out from a building. Assorted homeless cronies lounged on the sidewalk nearby. She approached me with open arms. My daughter, Lesley, cringed as we hugged. She was afraid of Michelle and backed away when I introduced them. When Michelle wasn't in earshot, Lesley said Michelle drank when I met her and she'd drink for the rest of her life. Why did I bother?

"Dig in, guys," my son, Greg, said when he put the box of clothing on the sidewalk.

Clothes flew through the air. Eugene held up Greg's leather-trimmed jacket, clutched it to his chest and smiled.

"That's mine," Michelle said and grabbed it.

Eugene ended up with a green jogging suit, which he stuffed into his belt for safekeeping. Muskrat put on a tweed jacket and light-brown woolen pants. He found a pair of high-top leather shoes, which he exchanged for his ripped sneakers. It was fitting attire for an Irish gentleman, even with his runny nose. He then turned the empty box upside down. When he sat on it, the box caved in. Muskrat landed on the sidewalk. But he was fortified with enough booze not to notice. Philip lay next to a building, resting his head on one hand to watch the commotion. He was too drunk to look through the clothing.

"Veggin' out today, Philip?" I asked.

"Hey, Judy. How you doin'?" he slurred.

It was unusually warm for a Sunday in March. People on their way to Central Park smiled at us. Rollerbladers with Spandex pants and helmets looked as they whizzed by. A vendor roasting peanuts watched the spectacle between sales. Michelle and her buddies gulped down more Thunderbird wine. It was a glorious day for them.

I took Michelle aside. "Why haven't you called your mother?"

"I'm sorry. I fell asleep on the subway. I'll do it tomorrow."

"You'll do it now. Call her from that payphone on the corner. No one from your family is coming to get you. I'm taking you to Italy in four days."

She stared at me with her mouth slightly open.

"That's right, you're going with me. Our tickets are waiting at the Alitalia Airline office on Fifth Avenue. The Italian Consulate's office has your travel documents. If you don't want to go, call your mother right now and tell her." No more saying she wanted to go home. This was our moment of truth. Either she went or she didn't. I looked at my mother who was watching us intently.

"Mom, talk to Michelle like a mother would talk to her daughter in a situation like this."

"Your mother gave birth to you. Go home. She doesn't care what you look like. You can't live like this on the street," she said.

I didn't believe Mother's *she doesn't care what you look like.* My mother had already formed a callous opinion about Michelle before they met. I knew my mother well, having felt her wrath for years, especially when I divorced and moved away from Rhode Island. I knew that look of disgust, combined with a rigid moral judgment.

I should have remembered my early days of knowing Michelle when I foolishly told my mother about her giving oral sex to a black man on the sidewalk. I knew better than to discuss sex with my mother. As soon as the words passed my lips, I regretted them. Mother led a monastic life after her divorce, choosing to sleep in a single bed. After my divorce, I continued in a bed for two and not always a bed at home.

"You're an adulterer," she'd accused me often. "You broke your marriage vows."

"So did you when you divorced."

"I divorced your alcoholic father because he said it'd be a cold day in Hell before he'd join AA. I wouldn't bring you up in an alcoholic home. My divorce was a civil action. In the eyes of the Catholic Church, I'm still married. I continue to practice my marriage vows today. You're divorced, too, and your marriage vows remain," she reminded me.

The day Mother met Michelle at the Chase bank and where I insisted she call her mother in Italy, I sensed Mother's standoffish behavior. Perhaps that's why I asked her to encourage Michelle. When she did, Michelle walked to the telephone, dialed the operator and gave her mother's number as a collect call. She swayed as that morning's booze took hold.

"Motherfucker," she said and slammed down the phone.

"Whoa, Michelle, What's the matter?" I asked.

"It's going click, click, click. I can't get through."

"Let me try," I said and dialed the operator. I repeated the telephone number and told Michelle to be patient. My six-foot-tall boys moved closer to us. My daughter couldn't take it anymore. She left. My mother watched from the sidelines. When I heard the international ring, I told Michelle the call was going through.

"*Pronto*," said a woman's voice on the other end.

"*Pronto*," I repeated.

Michelle jumped, as if prodded by an electrical device. She shook and grabbed the receiver.

"*Pronto! Mamma*," she sobbed and leaned against the booth's wall. She stuck a dirt-laden finger into one ear to block street noise. Tears streaked her swollen face. "*Mamma, sì, sì. È Mireille, sì Mamma.*"

The brief conversation was in Italian and French. When Michelle hung up, she smiled the sweetest smile I'd ever seen on her face.

"Well?" I said, barely able to speak due to the lump in my throat.

"I'm going home, Judith."

I looked at my boys. I bit my bottom lip, which was quivering, and gave them the thumbs-up sign. But Greg was looking elsewhere.

"Oh my God," he said, doubling with laughter. He pointed at Philip. "If only I had a camera. This is real New York."

We looked to the side of the bank where Philip stood, one hand against the building. His other hand held his penis. A stream of urine ran down the sidewalk as a bus stopped curbside and passengers stepped off. Philip righted himself and waved.

"How ya doin', ladies?" he said, as the stream flowed. "This here's hot soup."

Michelle didn't pay attention to him. Instead, she bent over and removed one of her red boots. At its bottom were six one-hundred-dollar bills, which she stuffed into my pocket. Philip had given her his $1,000 but they'd already spent some of it.

My birthday party later that day was just grand. Michelle, although absent, gave me the best present when she called her mother. Four more days and we'd fly over the Atlantic. But how I'd do it all alone was a nagging worry despite my good organizational skills. Since I had little supervision from the age of six because my mother worked full time, making decisions and doing what I wanted had been ingrained early in my life. Common sense, trusting my judgment and figuring out a situation independently were attributes I now had to apply to the monumental task of moving Michelle out of one country and into another.

Before Paolo's call, I'd been sent to the offices of Hadassah to type letters for a tree-planting campaign in Israel. The Jewish women's charitable organization had close ties with the country. The stuffy and crowded office on West 58th Street was near the Italian Consulate, Alitalia Airline and St. Patrick's Cathedral, which I'd visit on my lunch hour. My boss glared at me when I returned to my desk five or ten minutes late. I didn't reveal my charitable mission with Michelle. She'd never believe the details. Now I'd have to ask for time off.

Once I could see us leaving New York, I became terrified whenever I thought I'd have to bring Michelle to my home. She'd need to clean up, sleep on my sofabed and, most likely, I'd have to ply her with alcohol. She needed passport photos. We had appointments to keep. One slipup and there wouldn't be a second chance. I hated the responsibility. And I was annoyed with the Turoldos for dumping Michelle on me, even though I had suggested the trip. I weighed telling Paolo someone had to step in.

But during my birthday party, I looked at my four grown children, admiring each for their individuality. In the face of 23-year-old Dean Albanese, the second oldest, was the answer to my dilemma. He'd fly on the $100 Alitalia Airline companion ticket.

"Dean, want to go to Italy with me?" I asked.

"Sure I do. Are you kidding, Mom?"

"Nope. I need your help. Return to Rhode Island, pack and come back in two days."

"I'm ready. I can handle her. Thanks."

"Actually, I should thank you."

I went to the bank that night and brought Michelle some birthday cake. She was jubilant about our upcoming trip and for having spoken to her mother. "You're going to love my family," she said.

"I asked Dean to accompany us."

"He's coming? Wow. I like him. He's good looking."

"Get your Italian birth certificate from Eddie's apartment. Today is Sunday. Tuesday night, Dean and I will come to the bank. You'll clean up and stay overnight in my

Dean Albanese, Judith's son, March 1991

place. We have errands for Wednesday. We fly Thursday. And lighten up on the drinking."

"I'll do everything you say. I love you, Judith."

Walking home, I reasoned it was best she sleep in the bank lobby. What difference would two more nights make? I wanted her to be with Philip and the other street people. I had to be a dangling carrot. However, after I left Michelle eating my birthday cake seated on a urine-stained mattress, more drinking occurred that would endanger our trip.

the
media
loves us

WHEN MY PARTY ENDED, I KNOCKED on my neighbor's
door to return the pie server I'd borrowed. Irma Lazos was
an energetic young woman with large almond-brown eyes.
She was also an associate producer with *20/20*, the prime-
time ABC news magazine program.

"How are you, Judith?" she asked when she opened
her door.

"Honestly, I'm exhausted. Do you know that young
homeless woman in our neighborhood? I've befriended her
for several years, hoping she'd get sober. This Thursday, my
son and I are taking her home to her family in Italy."

"This is a perfect *20/20* human-interest story. Can I
suggest it to my boss?" she asked with a touch of excitement
in her voice. "Timing is short but maybe it will work out."

"You're right. It's ideal for that show. But I'm super
busy tying up loose ends. Maybe *20/20's* involvement is too
close to departure but thanks for the compliment." Then I
hesitated and thought about the impact Michelle's and my
story could make. "OK, Irma, what the hell. Suggest it to

your boss. But I have to ask Michelle if she's interested. It's her story, too."

Irma called the next day with the *20/20* commitment in hand. She hoped my relationship with Michelle's homeless friends could convince them to go to JFK airport for the farewell. There would be a film crew there and one in Italy for the family reunion. Stone Phillips would interview me in my apartment and interview Michelle on the street. Karen Saunders would be the segment's producer.

"This is moving fast. It has a circus quality to it," I said.

"We'll do it just fine. Plans call for Stone and Karen to interview Michelle's family in Italy."

The introduction of the media made sense. Homelessness was a growing national problem. Perhaps my hands-on approach would encourage others to help someone out when they'd see the *20/20* story. The country needed a new focus on the problem. I thought about the monumental expense the homeless accounted for in New York. Michelle's Medicaid bills were out of sight. Ambulances, hospitals, lab tests, the list was endless. Getting her out of New York doubled as a public service.

꒰m꒱

Monday night, three days before departure and my phone rang. "Judith, it's Michelle. I'm afraid. Can you get me now?"

"Where are you?" It was the first time she'd called my home.

"I'm with Eddie at the Chase bank. I have my birth certificate. I'm afraid," she whispered. "I can't find Philip or Eugene. I can't be out here alone."

Earlier that day, I'd accepted a last-minute ticket for a Carnegie Hall concert. It was close to curtain but I told her to wait. She was drinking from a bottle inside a paper bag when I arrived. Eddie was at her side. She looked presentable wearing Greg's jacket with my white sweater underneath.

"Can she stay with you?" Eddie asked. "She caused problems the last time at my place. My neighbors complained. I have to go to the city housing authority for a hearing. I can't bring her to my apartment tonight. She can't stay on the street without Eugene or Philip. Please, Judith, can she stay with you?" A look of despair crossed his face.

I didn't know what to say. But I still didn't want her in my home. Was I a hypocrite? My street compassion for her was genuine; I told our story to many people with conviction, enjoying praise given for my courage, but I couldn't take her home when she needed me.

"Not tonight, Michelle. I'm going to Carnegie Hall now. My date and I will go back to my place." I lied because I didn't want her in my apartment until Dean arrived the next day. "Can she stay with you one more night, Eddie?" I asked, now with despair in my eyes.

He looked at me and then at Michelle. "Do you promise to be good, Marie? No fights. No noise. Will you walk quietly up the stairs?"

"I promise."

"This will be our last night together."

"Only one more night on your own, Michelle. Dean arrives tomorrow. We'll come to the bank at 10:00 p.m. Start saying goodbye to your friends now, and lighten up on the booze."

Eddie reached for the paper bag in her hand. "You don't need to drink tonight."

"Don't fuck with me. I'll buy another one," she said and clutched the bag closer.

"I've got to go too, Michelle. You're safe with Eddie tonight."

As I walked away, I glanced over my shoulder. Michelle limped down West 57th Street holding her arm at the elbow. Eddie's feet turned outward, as he walked with a slight Charlie Chaplain bounce. He played a harmonica, which was a Christmas gift from Michelle. The Beatles "Imagine" trailed after them. I didn't like lying and pawning her off on Eddie, but what was the difference between that night and others? We weren't on that plane, yet.

The coordination of the trip with Michelle's family, dealing with the Consulate's office, Alitalia, the unexpected input of the *20/20* team, Michelle and her homeless gang, plus keeping up with my life as a temp secretary at Hadassah, took its toll. I was bone-weary and disheartened being desperately alone as the contact person for Michelle's survival. Not caring if she lived or died, despite visits to St. Patrick's Cathedral where I prayed for additional strength and patience, crept into my mind daily. What counteracted my thoughts was the hope I saw in her eyes.

Dean arrived Tuesday afternoon. He was upbeat. People in Rhode Island couldn't grasp homelessness in New

York, much less his role to take Michelle home to Italy. But I knew he had the perfect temperament to mingle with the homeless. He was tall, strong, stoic, lean and the more independent of my children. What some people didn't know was Dean had an enormous heart and could feel another person's pain.

He'd been a rebellious teenager and didn't shy away from a physical fight. With his towering frame and smart-aleck wits, Dean bullied people he thought bullied other people, viewing himself as a protector of the weak.

His brother Greg was two years older. They fought mercilessly as youngsters, only to turn into teenage confidants who smoked pot, drank alcohol, bunked school and chased girls. Greg was known for buying junk cars; he had 14 by the time he was 18.

"Just bought another $50 special, Mom," Greg said one day after he drove another heap into the driveway. I knew its hood would be open for a few hours while he tinkered with the engine. Once he tied a clothesline onto one wiper blade, ran it through the car and attached the end to the other wiper blade. When it rained, he'd manually pull the clothesline from inside the car to operate the wipers.

I'd been a single mother for about four years when Greg and Dean were in their roaring teens. Their school grades were mediocre, and they spent a lot of time outside the home. They couldn't conform to anyone's opinion but their own. They also made their own money with part-time jobs. Their father wasn't around that much, except to pick them up Sunday afternoons. Somehow I always trusted my boys to take care of themselves. No one messed with the Albanese boys. And everyone wanted to be their friend.

An alternative high school readied Dean for graduation. That day, he wore a black leather jacket, Grateful Dead T-shirt and tight black jeans. His knee-high moccasins had fringe running down the back. Flowing, wavy, dark-brown locks rested on his shoulders. He was bearded and wore reflective sunglasses.

By 21, he was an apprentice carpenter, clean-cut, well-dressed and lived with a girlfriend. Always independent, Dean couldn't be pushed into conformity. I liked his style. He adored me, my courage to change my life and sought my counsel with late-night calls.

Dean at 23 was perfect to accompany Michelle and me to Italy. We'd been to Spain a few years ago, so I knew his passport was current. He was also laid off due to the deep recession that affected the construction industry in the Northeast. When he arrived in New York, eager to go to Italy, we walked to the bank that night. I was ecstatic. I could finally bring Michelle home. My son would protect us.

"There she is, Dean," I said, pointing to Michelle's grubby red boots I saw through the bank's plate-glass window. What happened to the clean sneakers she'd worn the night before? She lay on the floor, lifeless, with Philip beside her. Eugene opened the door. His body shook, he was so happy to see us.

Muskrat sat on a window ledge still decked out in my son's donated clothes. He began to cry. "I know it's best for Michelle to go home, but I'll miss her. I love her, Judith," he sniffled. "I feel great in these clothes your boys gave me. I want to go home, too. Will you take me?"

"Not this time," Dean answered for me and gave him a few dollars.

I bent over Michelle, grabbed her boot and shook it. I said Dean and I were there to take her to my apartment. She could sleep in a bed that night. We were bound for Italy in a few days.

No response.

Dean knelt on one knee and touched her body. He, too, asked her to wake up. He shook her shoulder. She squirmed. She finally awoke, drunk and moaning in pain. Philip didn't move. She tried to get up but couldn't raise herself. Dean slid his long arms under her back and encircled her waist. She used them as a wedge and slowly inched upward.

"My shoulder hurts so bad," she cried out. "Eugene beat me the night you brought me birthday cake. He wanted to have sex but I wouldn't," she confessed to us.

Through the years, Michelle had been beaten, raped, robbed and manhandled. There was always a physical complaint but I knew this one was real. Maybe that's why she held her arm the night before when she walked to Eddie's apartment. Why didn't she say something then?

Walking to my apartment house, I regretted that I'd left her at the bank on Sunday night. Eugene was docile. Why did he beat her? His act solidified my fear about being alone with alcoholics who could get violent.

"I look like hell," Michelle said as she passed my lobby's full-length mirrors with Dean and me. When she entered my apartment, she said, "Ah, I'm finally home."

THE STREET OR ME

"This one is temporary. One more night and you'll be with your family," Dean said, as he slipped off Greg's oversized jacket she wore continually.

Michelle grimaced, held one arm in a bent position and looked at me.

"Sit anywhere you want," I said.

She chose a cream-colored velvet armchair. I wondered if her jeans were filthy on the rear. Dean gave her a pillow to rest her arm. He then poured her a glass of leftover punch from my party.

"We need to discuss something before you go home," I said, choosing my words carefully about the *20/20* segment. I told her it would be beneficial for Americans to see an authentic homeless person's life. I didn't want to highlight her downfall; I wanted to show how one person, an untrained person like me, could make a difference.

"How do they know about you and me?"

"My neighbor works on the show. Can I invite her over now?"

"Sure. Why not?"

Irma greeted Michelle warmly, but I sensed a judgment call being made with her quick visual assessment. She asked Michelle how she became homeless.

"When I met my deceased husband, Steve, he had money. We lived in Texas and went places. We drank and did drugs, too. One day, we're on the New York streets with nowhere to sleep. I wasn't brought up to be a homeless woman in the States or anywhere else. I have a wonderful family. I had a terrific childhood and wanted for nothing.

When I arrived in New York and saw the homeless people, I was afraid of them. Now I'm one, too."

"Have you seen *20/20?*" Irma asked and described the show's interest in our story.

"I want money to film me. I don't want to be exploited for your ratings."

"It's not ABC's policy to pay. It's a news program."

It took some convincing but Michelle agreed our story could be filmed without payment. She hoped there would be greater understanding of the homeless problem. But as the alcohol wore off, she squirmed in the chair, favoring her arm, only to let out a shriek when it slipped from the armrest.

"I'm not comfortable with this arm problem, Michelle. You should be seen at the hospital," I said, fearing the trip was in jeopardy.

Michelle loved medical attention and agreed.

Remembering Dr. Fischer, I paged him. It was around midnight.

"You got him," was his familiar response when I verified his name.

"It's Judith Glynn, the woman helping Michelle Browning. I'm taking her home to Italy in two days. I planned to call you about her medical records and a letter from you but there's a problem tonight."

"Whatever you need, I'll prepare. But what's up now?"

I explained Michelle's latest predicament. "Can she be seen now?"

"Is she with you?"

"Yes. She's in my apartment."

"Nail everything down. Don't let her out of your sight. Hide the booze. She's unconscionable. Is she near you?"

"Yes."

"OK. Bring her in. I'll get the shoulder X-rayed."

Dean and I walked Michelle to Roosevelt Hospital. She was melancholy about leaving New York. She loved America and never wanted to return to Italy. But she knew she was dying. Maybe she could get well in Italy and return. Maybe she became an American citizen when she married Steve.

As we waited for her to be seen in the emergency room, Michelle became agitated. "I need Phenobarbital. I'm shaking. I need a drink. You have no idea how horrible the DTs are," she told Dean and me. She paced nervously as the wait to see a doctor stretched on. "Look at me," she said with an outstretched arm that shook uncontrollably.

This was the first time Dean and I had witnessed alcohol-withdrawal. Michelle couldn't sit still and resembled a bird jumping from branch to branch. Finally, an intern arrived and escorted Michelle into an examination room where she screamed in pain when he removed her sweater. Dean and I eavesdropped as she explained the injury and her alcoholism.

The X-rays revealed she had a broken clavicle and badly bruised shoulder area. Normally, the injury required a sling and discharge, but she was sinking into severe alcohol withdrawal. Phenobarbital was pricked into her veins. She was admitted to the hospital for five days. Hopefully she'd detoxify and live.

"Dean, what about the trip?" I cried out when I heard the news. I expected her to fly semi-drunk. But how effective were five days' detox in a hospital ward? All plans needed to change. I hated Michelle just then. She was a selfish, ungrateful drunk who had succeeded in completely screwing up my life. And I hated myself, too. What a mess.

vigil keepers

KAREN SAUNDERS, THE *20/20* PRODUCER, went to Michelle's hospital bedside to confirm she could communicate well enough to be filmed. Michelle asked her if she could visit Steve's gravesite before she returned to Italy.

"It's a heartwarming request that could work with the story," Karen told me. "We'll go to Kentucky, stay overnight, return to Kennedy airport in New York and film her departure to Italy. What do you think?"

"Think? That's a grueling schedule. She's too ill to travel like that."

"I'll talk to Steve's family," Karen said, overlooking my concern.

Steve's parents had divorced, and they blamed Michelle for his death. They refused the interview. His grandmother had stopped accepting Michelle's collect calls, but would cooperate with 20/20. When Karen told Michelle we'd fly to Kentucky, she clutched the cross that hung around her neck given to her by Steve.

The ABC network contacted the Italian Consulate's office in New York and the Turoldo family in Italy. A relative, Antonio Sotille, was the family spokesperson, although he didn't speak English.

When Dean and I went to Michelle's hospital floor after she was admitted, she hovered over the nurses' station, demanding her medication before schedule. When she learned Phenobarbital would be stopped because it was toxic for her liver, she became argumentative and threatened to walk out.

"How about I have your clothes cleaned for the trip?" Dean asked Michelle when we returned to her room. He told me that he wanted to limit her access to clothing, although she'd left the hospital before in a hospital gown.

"Keep this for me," she said and gave Dean $80 she'd hidden in her pillowcase. Now she was penniless and without clothes but she'd escaped from the hospital before under similar circumstances.

Dr. Fischer visited her often. "I'll tie you down if you go near that elevator," he threatened. "Listen to Judith and stay away from those guys," he added, pointing to Philip and Eugene. "Don't end up like Steve. This is your last chance to live. Not one more drop."

He told Dean and me that Michelle was having hallucinations. She saw Steve sitting on the floor eating his shoe. Little red devils ran around her bed. She had nightmares and would awake screaming. She continually threatened to walk out.

"I'm going to appear on *20/20* with Barbara Walters," Michelle told the nurses.

They noted in her chart that her hallucinations continued with now a TV program filming her. When they learned Michelle Browning would be on *20/20*, they were wide-eyed.

On day three, Michelle showed improvement. The hospital barred Philip and Eugene from visiting her, fearing they'd bring in alcohol or drugs. I asked to reverse that restriction. Michelle needed them. Their presence and encouragement about Italy would keep her hospitalized. The next day they were back in her room. She was calmer.

Philip covered his stinking feet with a towel hoping to trap their odor. It didn't work. The stench permeated the room. The other patients complained to the nurses who could do nothing but commiserate. As he passed the hours in Michelle's warm room, he'd nibble from her food tray. Sometimes he'd pick at body lice and squash them on the arm of the chair.

"Did you get it, Philip?" Michelle asked and went about shaving her legs without lotion. Many times, she'd rub her face with hand cream, massaging it into the pores while she closed her eyes. Her expression was dreamlike.

Dawn was one of her roommates. She was a scrawny, toothless, crack addict, somewhere in her thirties. Her mousy-brown hair was clumped in spots. The pupil in one brown eye was foggy. She talked constantly, once proudly claiming to be a former prostitute, although I doubted the *former*. She wanted to change her life like Michelle was doing.

"I went to bed with lots of military men," she yelled across to me one day as I sat at Michelle's bedside. "You'd be surprised who runs this country and how I knew them."

The next day her bed was empty.

"Where's Dawn?" I asked Michelle.

"She bolted last night. Didn't say anything, just left," Michelle said, raising her shoulders up and down. The only trace of Dawn was her smelly clothing, a dead battery-operated radio and a plastic purse with a pair of broken sunglasses inside. Michelle had already bought her leather boots for $5. She'd wear them to Italy.

Overnight, Michelle was the center of attention on the ward. Most of the staff knew her and few believed she'd leave her addiction and New York. Dean and I wondered, too.

"Judith," she called after me when Dean and I were leaving one day. "Take me home with you right now because they're going to tie me up."

"Hold on, Michelle," I said over my shoulder. "Only a few more days and you'll be released. Don't tempt me to walk away from you for good. I'm at my breaking point. It's not all about you."

On another day, Michelle hugged me as I prepared to leave and put her hands on my rear. "You've got a nice ass," she said and rubbed her pelvic bone against mine.

"I'm not into women, Michelle, and you're not either," I said, as we laughed.

"You've said you hate me. I can't stand it when you say that. Do you hate me, Judith? Tell the truth."

"Sometimes."

"There's a reason we met. Don't forget that," she reminded me.

What pleased me most about Michelle's changing persona and sobriety was to hear her talk more about reuniting with her family. She saw a hospital in Italy with flowers around her bed and nice nurses. It was a place without security guards. She saw the canals of Venice and the farmlands around her home. And she cried often about her mother seeing her condition.

I relied upon Dean to placate Michelle while I worked during the day. He sat at her bedside and listened patiently to her babble. He gave her back rubs, lit her cigarettes and held her hand whenever they walked in the corridor. I'm convinced she stayed in the hospital partly because of his devotion.

When he was a teenager in Rhode Island, he worked nights at a downtown restaurant and would feed a few bums, as they were called in those days, from the back door. Dean was tough on the outside but a compassionate softie inside. But the instant love and devotion to Michelle's well-being was different, especially for someone his age. To be thrown into the New York City homeless subculture and adjust without judgment was commendable.

"What do you see in her, Dean?" I asked.

"There's still a touch of class left. I think she can be pretty someday."

"I think she's pretty now. Maybe I've adjusted my opinion of beauty."

"There's something very addictive about her personality that draws people to her."

Day four of Michelle's stay was like the others when I'd visit. It was boring, centered on her but with an occasional laugh. She was sober, in command and knew what was happening. My one pleasure was to see her become childlike when we discussed Italy. Philip would listen, looking sad. But he was out of money and looked to me for help.

"Judy, would you ask Marie for some money?" he said when she went to the bathroom. "I need money real bad."

We all knew Michelle controlled their purse strings with a tight rein. However, all their money was at my apartment as we awaited her discharge and upcoming trip. She'd given me $600 the day we called her mother, and she gave Dean another $80 stuffed in her hospital pillow.

"How much?" I asked.

"Shit, man, I need at least $8," he said, lowering his head and pulling his cap down.

When Michelle returned from the bathroom and hopped on her bed, Philip and I stared at her.

"Philip needs money," I said matter-of-factly. "Can I give him some from the money you gave me to hold?"

"How much does he want?" she asked, ignoring Philip.

"Eight dollars," I said.

Michelle jerked her head in his direction. Her eyes squinted. Her lips pursed. "Five dollars only," she answered sternly.

"What?" I gasped, caught up in Philip's plight. "That's nothing. He needs more than five."

Philip remained silent and avoided our eyes.

"Five is all he gets. He'll drink the rest."

"Five it is, Philip. Sorry about that."

"Damn," he said and shook his head. He pulled his hat down even lower, folded his arms and slumped in his chair. "Damn, Marie, I need more than five dollars."

"Only five. Now shut up," she said.

I handed Philip the money. He stuffed it into his jean pocket. And that was that.

<m>

One day during Michelle's hospitalization, a *20/20* film crew set up the interview between Stone Phillips and me at my apartment. Rugs were rolled up; furniture rearranged and pictures removed from the wall. Lights and sound levels were tested. Finally, two chairs were plopped in front of my fireplace.

"You must be Judith," said a man as he approached with his hand extended in a handshake.

Stone Phillips, the *20/20* correspondent, was handsome. I liked the sincere look in his eyes, which convinced me the interview would go well. And it did, for two hours. When he left my apartment briefly and before he and I were to walk along Eighth Avenue to relive my street life with Michelle, I telephoned Dr. Fischer to confirm her release. Stone and Karen were flying to Italy and needed to interview her either in the hospital or at my place before their departure.

"She's not being released tomorrow," Dr. Fischer said with conviction. "I think she's drunk herself into the grave this time. She's in liver failure. Her ammonia level is too high. That's why she continues to hallucinate. The level has to decrease in the next 48 hours or she'll die."

I was crestfallen. We were days from a new beginning in Italy. How could she die now?

"Great interview, Judith," Stone said when he returned to my apartment. He loved the story and was anxious to interview Michelle.

"Dr. Fischer just called. Michelle is in liver failure. She may not make it. The next 48 hours are crucial."

Dean was in the room listening to the events unfold. When he heard Michelle might die, he put on his jacket and said he was going to her bedside.

Rather than cancel the *20/20* day completely, the crew filmed Stone and me walking along Eighth Avenue. We stopped at the convenience store where Michelle was a daily pest and in the apartment vestibule where she gave me permission to write to her mother. At 10:00 p.m., Karen and I were at the bank to film Philip, Eugene and the other homeless.

At first, Philip wanted money for ABC's exploitation of him. He didn't want the Chase sign shown. Why should they get free publicity? Karen said Michelle and he were the perfect spokespeople for the homeless. He finally agreed.

The day ended at midnight with hours of footage in the can. The producers talked about the segment in terms of an award-winning piece. I was pleased, too, but my thoughts were with Michelle. If need be, I'd sit at her bedside around the clock and will her to live. She'd obviously chosen me over her street life. I couldn't abandon her now.

The phone rang early Tuesday morning. Dean and I were sleeping late and let the recorder pick up the call.

"Judith, I'm sending Eugene to your house to get my clothes. Give him the money. I don't have a penny in my pocket. I hate this hospital," Michelle said.

"Dean, get up and talk to her," I called to him.

He bolted out of bed and picked up the phone. "Hey, hon, how you doing? Listen, I was just on my way over there." Pause. "Can't bring your clothes. They're in the cleaners." Pause. "We'll talk when I get there."

Dean pulled on his clothes, splashed water on his face, gulped down orange juice, lit a cigarette and headed for the door. He'd try to stop her, although she was determined to walk out of the hospital that day.

The bad news about Michelle was good news for *20/20*. Each day she stayed in New York made the coordination of the trip to Italy easier. Karen asked the hospital's public relations department if they'd allow a film crew in Michelle's room. They refused, which surprised Karen and me. Michelle was a neighborhood pest who soiled their emergency room for years and received free medical care. She was verbally and physically abusive to the staff. Her story was worth telling but I guessed they didn't think so.

I'd learn later some hospital personnel believed I wanted a media event. I wondered if they would have accompanied me through the dark streets for the years it took to help her.

Michelle's health changed hourly as did our departure plans. The Kentucky trip to Steve's gravesite was cancelled.

She had to get to Italy immediately, if and when her ammonia level dropped.

"It's a good thing Michelle has to stay in the hospital a few more days," Karen said. "That helps us with Italy." That statement, said to me and later to *20/20*'s top management, turned into the death knell for the network's involvement with Michelle.

Unbeknownst to Dean and me as we talked to Michelle about the segment, a meeting was underway at ABC to discuss its future. Company policy and news' ethics surfaced when Karen said it was a good thing Michelle had to stay in the hospital. That was interpreted by top brass as a suggestion Michelle *should stay* in the hospital longer to enable the producer and reporter to reach Italy before she did.

When the log for the story was reviewed, the numerous changes that dated back to the trip Karen planned to Steve's gravesite and family in Kentucky further influenced their decision. No one wanted to be scrutinized if the story looked staged. There appeared to be nuances of changing reality. *20/20* only did stories as they happened and were real. The segment was cancelled.

"Karen, what do you mean *cancelled*?" I said when she told me. "How can I tell Michelle and the homeless at the bank? What about her family in Italy? Cancelled because of a stupid reason? It's a great story for the public to see."

ABC's decision didn't make sense. A TV producer couldn't influence a medical decision to keep Michelle in the hospital.

"I can't remember a segment being cancelled, especially with so much footage shot. They spent a lot of money on it," Irma said in exasperation.

"I'll tell Michelle if you want," Karen said in a strained voice. Although a company lady, this one didn't settle well with her.

"I'll tell her."

I didn't. Instead, Dean and I babysat to keep Michelle in the hospital bed. She'd been there eight days and was fidgety. Her ammonia level was still high. Philip sensed our fear that Michelle would back out. Whenever she wanted out of the hospital, he'd say she had to stay. He loved Michelle, yet was pushing her away to save her life. His homeless friends told me he cried at night because he wanted her beside him.

Eddie Benson was a daily visitor to Michelle's room. He'd rush in, sometimes twirl around and around until he stopped at her bed. He'd cup her face and lean in to kiss her, but she'd pull away. He said his prayer group prayed three times a week for her health and to return to her mother.

"Judith, I'm dizzy," he complained to me, gripping his head with his dirty hands. "I can't walk straight," he said weaving across the room, feigning lightheadedness.

Michelle kept him running between his apartment and her hospital room. She wanted her clothes, shoes, makeup and stuff that was piled high in his spare room. Eddie brought back dribs and drabs, some in boxes or in a dilapidated 1940's suitcase.

"My mother would die if I go home carrying that. Throw it away," she said.

"Did you notice how the Devil brings me a few things at a time? Look at these fucked-up socks," Michelle said and held up a mismatched pair. "He thinks I can't live without him but now I can," she told Dean and me.

Late Wednesday evening, there was hope. Michelle's ammonia level began to drop. She talked to her mother again and that peaceful look crossed her face. Mrs. Turoldo said the family would meet her in Venice. Michelle hoped she'd recognized them.

So many times I wanted the Turoldo family to relieve me of this outrageous responsibility I'd heaped on myself. When Michelle's hospitalization almost cancelled the trip, where were they? They couldn't be that naïve as to not understand my burden. But her family never mentioned taking over. As deep as Michelle was into her alcoholism, I was getting in deeper helping her.

Michelle, Philip, Eugene, Dean and I went to the hospital's communal reception area one last time, as visiting hours drew near their close. She'd be released the next morning. The hospital was preparing her records for me to take to the Italian doctors, along with Dr. Fischer's promised letter. I'd also be responsible for doling out her tranquilizers and pain pills needed for the shoulder injury. Although the shakes had stopped, Michelle was very nervous. So was I. Our flight to Italy was confirmed for two days later — March 15th, at 6:30 p.m. It would be a momentous day. It was also my birthday.

Philip was gallant and led Michelle by the elbow to a chair in the reception area. As she sat down, he put one arm behind his back and bowed in front of her. "I can't take it when you ladies get together and talk," he said with a grin and moved away to sit with Eugene, as I sat down beside Michelle.

A patient nearby covered her nose with a towel. "Are you a patient here?" she asked Philip.

"Are you kidding? Dressed like this?"

The woman got up and left the room.

Michelle liked the textured stockings I wore that night. And when I hiked my skirt to show her the full effect, she hiked her pajama pant legs to show me her legs. "They used to be better. But see, they're straight."

To have her notice fashion and to look at herself from a female perspective was a major accomplishment for me. Little by little, Michelle Browning was becoming a lady again.

With the eight-day hospital stay about to end, she confessed to Dean and me that she wanted to walk out many times. In the past, no one paid attention if she did. This time it was different. She couldn't do it to us. I was so proud of her and told her so. That led me to believe our presence was vital. What I didn't reveal to her was how often I was purposely late going to the hospital; it was an hour-by-hour stall tactic to keep her there, which worked.

"Where you been, Judith? I've waited eight hours for you," she scolded one day as her health steadily improved.

"Hey, listen to me, Michelle. I have a full life that doesn't include you all the time. I work every day, I cook for Dean and me at night, and I'm dealing with the authorities to get you home. Give me a break."

"I'm very sorry," she said and lowered her head.

Obviously, homelessness creates an unrealistic approach to how the stable world operates. For years, Michelle controlled her senseless days. She wasn't about to control mine. Also, I learned most conversations with a homeless person quickly turn monotonous. An addiction at her level had a strong grip, which produced an unwillingness to take stock. The outside world is perceived as cruel and non-caring.

However, on Michelle's last evening in Roosevelt Hospital, orderlies, nurses and aides called out good luck when they saw us sitting in the reception room. Even the social worker, one of her biggest skeptics, finally believed she'd go home. Michelle glowed saying her goodbyes.

a mother's scorn

I AWOKE SMILING. IN TWO DAYS, THE long, frightening, rewarding and remarkable time I spent with homeless Michelle Browning would end in Italy. She'd be Mireille Turoldo again.

Dean went to get coffee and bagels before we'd go to the hospital and sign Michelle's release papers. I decided to call my mother with a Michelle update. Maybe she'd be proud of her only child for undertaking a remarkable task, one which Stone Phillips and a major network thought worthy to film despite its cancellation.

"Hi, Mom, how's it going?" I asked when she answered. "I've got some exciting news for you."

"I thought I lost Ruben this morning," she said. "Looked all over my apartment and in the outside hallway. Couldn't find that damn cat. I was heartbroken. Then I heard this tiny meow coming from the closet. Sure enough, he was behind the door. How's that for a doozy of a story?"

"You and your cats," I said, hoping to change the subject. "After death, I want to return as your animal." I always thought she cared more for her two Persian cats and a Cocker Spaniel dog than she did for me, especially as I grew older and made decisions she challenged. After her death, I found the cats' birth certificates and lineage but not mine.

"Well, they've given me comfort for years. What did you want to tell me?"

"It's about Michelle. Stone Phillips from *20/20* was in my apartment and did an interview with me. Imagine that, Mother. Your daughter was going to be on national TV. The film crew followed us along Eighth Avenue and to the bank lobby to recreate my story with Michelle and her homeless friends. And you should see how wonderful Dean is with her. We fly to Italy in two days."

"I can't figure out why you bother with her." Mother's tone was cold.

"Huh? I didn't seek her out. This whole thing escalated as the years passed. When someone from Italy didn't come to take her home, I volunteered to do it. Now Dean's helping. What are you talking about *why did I bother with her?*"

"I know you," she said, as I envisioned her scowl. "You're doing this for publicity. You want to write a story. You can't fool me."

"You believe I'd be in the dangerous homeless culture for years just to write a story?"

"Yes, I do."

"Well, you're dead wrong. And why aren't you proud of me? Aunt Vera said your knitting group wants you to stop talking about me. They can't figure out why you're not proud of me. Look how I've improved my life compared to our beginnings."

"Your favorite Aunt Vera has plenty to say about everyone. That sister-in-law of mine rides her white horse all over town. What does she know about struggling to get by?"

"So what's your issue, Mother? What's really bothering you about Michelle and me? Spit it out." I could feel a lump develop in my throat. Why wasn't she ecstatic about the obstacles I'd jumped over to dismantle our humble beginnings? She could bask in my reflected glory, but she didn't. Oh, the damage her razor-sharp tongue and iceberg heart did to me through the years, enough to brace me for what was coming.

"My issue?" she shrieked. "Why didn't you see an issue with her when she gave oral sex to that black man on the sidewalk? Oh, no, you didn't see anything wrong now, did you? Drunk or not, homeless or not, she's a whore. But you'd understand that, wouldn't you?"

She knew that fact about Michelle because I'd told her, thinking Mother would be as disgusted as I about homelessness for women. Granted, Michelle lived a sub-human life and was surprisingly still alive after multiple years in the gutter, but whore she was not.

"Oh, so I'd understand what being a whore was like, right Mother? Just what do you mean by that zinger? Something bothering you about me that you'd like to discuss?"

"How soon you forgot your marriage vows after you divorced. You took right up with sleeping with other men. I'd call that a whore, too."

"How dare you call me that? I'm a grown woman and mother to the four grandchildren you adore. I've completely reinvented myself. I'm capable of making my own decisions and choosing my bed mate is one of them! Let's not go there again."

She remained silent.

"Obviously, there's nothing more to say. And you won't see me on *20/20* because the segment was cancelled. That should please you. And, may I add, Mother, you're an incredibly mean-spirited person. Can't you see beyond your repressed sexual upbringing that Michelle giving oral sex on a street has nothing to do with what I'm doing to take her home to her mother?"

"You can say whatever you want. You're in good company with her."

I hung up on my mother, leaned forward on the couch and put my head in my hands. Deep sobs came out of me. Nothing had prepared me for this searing conversation. Where and why had our relationship gone so wrong?

Among mankind, Mother was a full-blown character, someone who catnapped through life. She never appeared tired, depressed, sad or insecure. Ultimately, the ride we took was worth the adventure once I accepted the twisted and bitter woman I sensed controlled her inner self. Mother was a rarity, a phenomenon who overcame countless odds except her narrow judgment of me.

Divorce was unheard of in parochial Rhode Island in the 1950's when Mother divorced my alcoholic father. Without child support, she went to work full time as a secretary, leaving me to climb many a back staircase to enter our one-bedroom apartment with a dog and a cat waiting. She moved 50-plus times throughout her lifetime, dragging me along for about half and until I married. The majority of apartments were in Providence's East Side neighborhood.

"These are my roots," she'd say referring to the area where she was born, not realizing — nor caring — that each displacement and new address ripped away any semblance of roots from under me.

Our nomadic lifestyle was anchored in packing boxes, rolled up rugs, furniture to fill four rooms and household items hastily thrown into any container. Ketchup, a loaf of bread and an iron would share space with bedroom slippers. Dishes were wrapped in clothes; a can opener would be mixed in with plastic hair rollers. A lamp shade transported towels. It all seemed normal, as did returning to the same street to live in a different apartment.

"I can move on my lunch hour," she'd say.

And she was correct. We had moved on her lunch hour.

Mother had a great sense of humor, which often masked the cruelty of her comments. She was an intelligent, independent woman, stoically confined to a typewriter to support us. When I entered high school and her well-off brothers wanted to send me to college, Mother refused. She said I'd be a secretary, which is what I became after graduation. But somewhere in my late-30s and after my divorce, my entrepreneurial spirit blossomed. I had numerous part-time jobs, ranging from survey taker outside of shopping malls, to restocking nail polish shelves in discount stores, to part-time secretary, to unpaid campaign worker in political campaigns, plus I was an unwavering helper at my children's school.

When I discovered I could write, I took a few college courses. And when I published, began to travel and set out alone, had I eclipsed Mother with my freelance life in business and in love? Had I absorbed her bravery that she despised in me because I'd succeeded with my lifestyle when she didn't take risks because of her social, religious and mental boundaries? Had I trumped her, which led to her festering distain for me? Was it jealousy?

But the final blow for us was when I left Rhode Island to survive mentally, spiritually and financially. Mother never acknowledged how despondent and long-suffering I'd been, or the courage it took to change my life for the better and for that of my children.

"You left before your daughter menstruated," she accused me when I returned once for a visit. "And you slept your way across Europe on those trips," she added.

"Not quite, Mother. Just Spain and Portugal," I responded, enjoying the verbal sparring.

By the time my life showed success, I'd purchased a home in New York, had put Derek through school and had terrific relationships with my other children. It seemed my choices had paid off. But I don't remember being complimented by Mother for my guts, which I knew I'd inherited from her.

As I waited for Dean to return with breakfast, I took one last sob and made a decision. I'd never talk to my mother again. I didn't have to love her. I didn't have to like her, either. And I didn't need her anymore. My life was content and complete with my family, a unit she could continue to adore but without me around.

"Have you been crying, Mom?" Dean asked when he came home. "Is Michelle OK?"

"It's not Michelle. Come sit beside me. It's your Nana. She called me a whore just like Michelle is. She said I'm helping her so I can write a story. We had a bad argument. I'll never talk to her again."

"Don't listen to her, Mom. That's another generation. I'm sure she loves you."

"She doesn't love me, Dean. I'm a mother and I'd never talk to my children that way. But she's been a wonderful Nana. Promise me what just happened won't harm how you feel about her." I leaned my head on his shoulder, thinking life was strange. I was my mother's wounded child at that moment, as my child comforted me as a mother would.

"I promise," he assured me.

"Here we're doing a good deed. Michelle's mother loves her despite her messed up life. She wants her home. And my mother hates me for taking her. Why?"

"We'll never know *why*. Forget it. You have to be strong to get Michelle on the plane. You made it this far. Dry your eyes and get dressed. Michelle is released today. Tomorrow is full of last-minute stuff. Then it's Italy the next day."

her last street day

DEAN AND I DRESSED MICHELLE SLOWLY and walked to the nurses' station where I signed her release papers. Our first stop was to fill her prescriptions and to take passport photos. The three of us took a cab to the Italian Consulate.

"I'll deduct this cab ride from your money," I told her. "No more freebies. You need to be responsible for yourself."

We were shown to a desk at the Consulate where the representative who helped me spoke to Michelle in English and in Italian. She had a displaced, dazed look. After she signed paperwork for her temporary passport, she stared at him in disbelief as tears dripped down her cheeks. I knew she'd have to file for new papers in Italy to return to the States. I'd promised her she could return. She probably could, but it wouldn't be easy. I sensed I'd betrayed her.

Our next stop was Alitalia Airline on Fifth Avenue. I made Michelle pay for that cab ride.

"Can I drink on the flight?" Michelle asked the clerk as she prepared our tickets.

"You've been sober for eight days. Be sober for your family when you arrive," I said.

"You said I could drink if I wanted to."

"We'll talk about that later." I had promised she could drink on the flight but that was before her hospitalization, before hallucinations and before possible liver failure.

"Is this a round trip ticket?" Michelle asked.

"Yes," the clerk answered and handed over the tickets with moistened eyes.

On the street again with all paperwork complete, Dean reminded Michelle we had a few hours before dinner, then bed, then Italy the next day. "Ready?" he asked and reached for her hand.

"I'm not sure," she said, staring straight ahead.

We decided to walk home, all of us needing the fresh air. Outside of Mariella's Pizza, across the street from where I'd first seen Michelle years before, she looked in the shop's window. She wanted to say goodbye to the staff.

Round disks of dough were twirled upward as we approached the counter. Tomatoes, cheese and baking crust aromas filled the air. When Giuseppe, the owner, saw Michelle, he stopped mid-throw to rest the dough on the counter and walked over to us.

"Eh, how you doing today, Marie?"

"I'm going home to Italy tomorrow."

"You shitting me?"

"I'm going with this lady and her son. Show him the ticket, Judith."

I put her ticket on the counter and pointed to Venice.

"You're going home to *Mamma*. Good for you. And don't get drunk or do drugs in Venice. Don't come back," he said. "Hey, send me your address. I'll visit you next time I'm in Italy."

I ordered a full-size pizza with extra cheese, and we waited for it at a marble-topped table.

"Hey, Giuseppe, I'm sorry for turning the tables upside down," Michelle said, as he inserted a long paddle into a hot oven to retrieve a pizza.

"That wasn't all you did in here. When my brother told you to leave, you grabbed the Christmas tree in the window and smashed it on the floor."

"I'm sorry about that, too. But it won't happen again."

When we left the shop, she stopped mid-block. She pursed her lips, squinted and panned the surrounding sidewalks. She turned herself around in a circle. She wanted to find Philip. My heart fluttered. I felt a sweat coming on. I envisioned her drinking with him. A feeling of defeat, confusion and despair always hovered as our trip neared.

"Let's look in the subway station," Dean suggested. "If he's not there, we'll walk around until we find him."

I desperately wanted Michelle in Italy, addiction in hand, and my life back. But the stress and pressure of Michelle's unexpected hospital stay, coupled with my escalating role of responsibility, had taken a toll on me. My complexion was pale, and I'd lost weight. I was exhausted, made worse by the hepatitis C virus I unknowingly carried.

From the beginning of our odyssey, I questioned my obsessive involvement with her. Why not let her die out there? Why was I the one who couldn't stop caring about her? Whenever I'd examine my motives that went unanswered, I wondered if Michelle was simply a project to complete. And when I began to write our story, was she nothing more than the subject of a great article? My mother's accusation never left me.

Our unusual friendship was an interesting conversation piece. Friends and acquaintances were drawn in when I'd show her photo and elaborate about us. Only a few expressed disgust at the homeless situation that had ballooned to unfathomable numbers throughout America. Everyone wanted to help in some way, but how? Or they were frightened. My story inspired hope. Many people diagnosed Michelle with AIDS. Responsibility for her plight was shifted to social agencies or back to her to cure herself. Few recognized that a non-professional, such as me, could change a homeless person's life. I was praised and told God would reward me. But most people cringed to think they could replicate the deed. As for AIDS, when I asked Dr. Fischer, he couldn't recall that as one of her medical problems. I thought it was a strange response but maybe she had so many afflictions he couldn't remember them all.

Everyone asked how she sank so low. I'd reveal what I knew. But it wasn't how she got there; she had to get out of homelessness, fast. I'd say I loved her. I admired her spunk. What resilience it took to sleep on the ground, night after night, drunk or sober. Where did she go to the bathroom? She had no future, no money, lice-ridden companions and was shunned by society. But she still lived, full of love for her husband and with a deep faith in God.

I couldn't stay away from her. She didn't need me, per se, she needed help. I was a bridge, a conduit to a final destination. Without her family in Italy as my goal, I doubted I would have stayed around. And if she died on the New York streets, at least she'd know someone cared at her lowest point. So I stayed in, grit my teeth and continued to close in on her addiction. Michelle Browning was going home regardless of what people thought of us. And we were one day away.

Michelle and Dean found Philip and they went to *The Doors* movie. She and Dean returned to my apartment as planned, and she was sober.

"Where do I sleep?" she asked, as we prepared for bed.

"On the pullout. If you want to use the bathroom, Dean and I will prepare the bed for you."

When she returned to the room, she lay down on the sofabed and covered herself with a fresh sheet and blanket.

Dean looked at her lying there and me in my bed. He'd need to inflate a portable mattress. "I'm sleeping here," he said and got in bed with Michelle, reaching for her hand.

"This is the first time you've slept in my home, Michelle," I said.

"What took you so long?"

"Hey, my mother had to work out a few things," Dean said in my defense.

She didn't answer; instead, she drifted off to sleep with a smile.

a gentleman named philip

"I'M NERVOUS ABOUT GOING HOME," Michelle said to me on departure day.

"Me too, but I've got something to tell you before we leave," I said.

"Is my mother mad at me?"

"Of course not. She wants you home. It's about the *20/20* program. I'm sorry to tell you the producers cancelled the segment."

"That's OK. Philip always said I can't trust anyone. But I feel bad for you. Many people tried to help me but I'd go back to the street. You're good at this."

I was furious with *20/20's* aloof style. How dare they commit, entice, intrude, abuse and walk away without a backward glance. Other than Karen's retreating call, no one offered an explanation or regret. But I'd grown to realize national media had an interest so I called a few newspapers.

The *New York Post* reporter Hope MacLeod interviewed Michelle and me by telephone on departure day. There wasn't much time before we'd leave for the airport, but could she send over a photographer? The story would appear in the next day's newspaper. Michelle agreed. She read the *Post* before she'd sleep on it and used it to blow her nose.

"Michael Schwartz from the *New York Post*," said the upbeat man when he entered my apartment. Cameras bumped against his chest. "She doesn't appear too fried after years on the street," he whispered to me. He liked our story.

One click into the photo session and Michael answered his beeper. "You ladies gonna be here for a little while? I have to cover a jumper at 56th Street and Ninth. Can I come back?"

We chuckled when he left. No one in media stayed around us too long.

Michael returned a short time later. "Nah, he wasn't even there when I arrived. Just a bunch of people looking up."

During the photo-taking session, my boss at Hadassah called. Despite my good deed of taking Michelle home, the office had to run and I took too much time off. She fired me.

"Tell that to the *Post* reporter," Michael said. "Someone will hire you. Here you're taking someone off the streets of New York, something many want to do, and you're fired because of it. Helluva city, isn't it?"

"No big loss," I said, but it would be to be unemployed when I returned.

Three hours before departure and the tension built in the apartment. I still wasn't packed, nor was Michelle.

NEW YORK POST, SATURDAY, MARCH 16, 1991 ★5

Good Samaritan saves ex-beauty queen from streets and gives her

A NEW LEASE ON LIFE

By HOPE MacLEOD

BELLE OF ITALY
Michelle Browning at 18.

A former Italian beauty queen who ended up an alcoholic panhandler living on the streets of New York is heading home for a new start — thanks to a caring passer-by.

"I think it's wonderful," 33-year-old Michelle Browning said of her benefactor's help. "I couldn't do it by myself.

"I was scared. I guess the Lord was with me, or I wouldn't be alive now," she said.

Good Samaritan Judith Glynn, a Manhattan publicist and tourism writer, said: "I accomplished what I set out to do — to give her hope."

The two, along with Glynn's 23-year-old son, Dean Albanese, were to fly from Kennedy Airport last night for Udine, Italy, and the loving arms of Browning's mother, three sisters and two brothers.

Two years ago, Glynn started noticing the petite blue-eyed brunette around the Columbus Circle area where she lives.

"She was obviously homeless, so young, so drunk," Glynn said. "I wanted to know more about her so, one day, I stopped and asked her name."

Months passed, wariness grew to trust and Browning started telling bits and pieces about her past:

Michelle, whose maiden name is Mirella Turoldo, was born of Italian parents in Dijon, France. When she was 18, she said, she won a beauty contest in Venice.

Later, a photographer lured her to Houston with promises of love and a modeling career. When that fell through, she traveled around the country and married Steve Browning, supposedly from a wealthy rifle manufacturing family in Virginia.

Eventually, they wound up in New York, broke and homeless.

"We were sleeping in the subway and getting beat up by people and cops," she said. "People called me a bum. I tried to get a job, but no one wanted me because I couldn't take a shower and wore the same clothes every day."

She said Steve died last

'A NEW LIFE': Michelle Browning (right), 33, with benefactor Judith Glynn yesterday.

November, apparently of acute alcoholism, and she wanted to commit suicide.

"I never brought her home," said Glynn. "I felt that was just a Band-Aid, to wash her up and send her back out on the street again. I wanted to offer her

hope."

A month ago Glynn wrote to Michelle's mother and enclosed a picture of her daughter as she is today. A nephew called back and said the family wanted her to come home and would pay for the trip.

"I'm very happy to go," Browning said. "I'm a little nervous about the way I look now. But yes, it will be a new life, definitely."

She looks forward to "just being a hairdresser" in Venice, a job for which she had been trained.

FIRST COMMUNION
12-year-old Michelle.

New York Post article - March 16, 1991

She took another long, hot shower, put the curling wand to three clumps of hair and gave up. She never had the haircut she wanted, and her long, stringy hair hung down her back. Nor did she buy a present for her mother or clothes for herself.

"I want to wear the white sweater you gave me. I love it," she said.

I pulled it gently over her head. Next, I pulled up her jeans with the bloodstained knee. Dawn's boots slipped easily up her calves. She borrowed a suitcase and wanted to stuff in all clothing from Eddie's apartment. Included was a shimmering cocktail dress, backless shoes, a stained white angora sheath and balls of outdated clothing. The stench was powerful.

Stressing baggage weight limits, Dean and I suggested she choose, but Michelle was incapable of choosing anything. Frustrated, Dean knelt down, picked up a few items and shoved them into the suitcase. He zippered it shut as the sides bulged.

"There, we're ready," he said, looking at me and the suitcase in disbelief.

"I'm tired," she said, not concerned about the luggage. "And I need my medicine. How about a double dose, Judith?"

"No way. A double dose could set us back. If you mess with me and this trip gets cancelled again, I'm gone from your life," I warned.

"I want to say goodbye to my friends," she said to Dean when there was a lull between packing and leaving for the airport.

"Go with her, Dean and be back at 4:00 o'clock," I said.

When they returned, Michelle was ghost-white. I was apprehensive; worried my quest to reunite Michelle with her family wouldn't happen. She'd go back to street life. Dean hurried us along as we gathered our suitcases and closed my apartment door behind us. He reminded me that Philip wanted to go to the airport with us.

"This is it, Michelle," I said and pressed the elevator button. My heart pounded in my ears. Perspiration formed under my armpits. My stomach knotted. My knees were weak. I didn't like nor trust her at that moment. I knew the powerful seduction of alcoholism. Would she escape once we reached the street?

"I won't go home without a pint of peach schnapps," Michelle mumbled behind me, as our suitcases rolled across the lobby's tile floor.

I didn't respond. Dean opened the front door, and we pulled our suitcases up several stairs. Once on the sidewalk, Michelle brushed past me, walking briskly toward Eighth Avenue.

"I won't go," she yelled over her shoulder and left her suitcase stranded on the sidewalk.

Tears rolled down my cheeks. "Dean, stop her," I pleaded.

His long legs quickened until he grabbed the arm of her jacket. "You're not going anywhere in New York. You're going to Italy. Get your suitcase," he ordered and led her back to the left luggage.

She obeyed. She then looked at me and saw my tears.

Philip and Eugene waited for us in front of McDonald's. Despite their disheveled, homeless look, I saw two gentlemen. When I shouted I needed them, Philip darted skillfully in and out of traffic on busy Eighth Avenue to reach Michelle, Dean and me. Eugene followed.

Michelle ran to Philip's side, crying hysterically. "I have to have a drink. I won't go without one. Please, Philip," she said as her body shook.

While she begged, Dean hoisted our suitcases into the trunk of a cab.

"Michelle, hurry up," I called to her. "We'll miss our flight. You can drink on the plane."

"It's too expensive," she said.

"I'll buy," I said, willing to promise anything.

She turned her back on me and ran down Eighth Avenue in the direction of the liquor store.

Philip followed and stopped her. "Marie," he said gently. "You're making Judy cry. I'll go to the airport with you."

She stopped in her tracks and hesitated. She looked at the liquor store two doors away, then at Philip, Eugene, Dean and me. Something clicked because she agreed to go to the airport without alcohol. She then shook Eugene's hand in farewell and kissed his cheek. He lowered his head and wished her good luck. Her anger at his beating was evident, but she was gracious at the end.

When the cab doors slammed shut, Michelle was in the back seat, trapped and dwarfed between Dean and Philip. I was in the front with the driver. I cracked the window open, hoping Philip's odor would escape. His conversation was lively about working at the airport. He was unusually open, a trait he'd hidden.

"Find a liquor store driver. Stop this cab," Michelle demanded.

I tapped the driver's knee and whispered to continue to the airport.

"Marie, baby. I don't see no liquor store around here. We're not stopping," Philip said.

As the miles whizzed by, I wondered what I'd done to Michelle, my son, her waiting family, to a rag-tag community of homeless nomads, to my family and friends, to Dr.

Fischer, nut-case Eddie Benson and all the kind-hearted people I'd encountered who moved mountains to get this drunk, smelly, ingrate of a homeless woman home to her family. This was all crazy, and I'd created the circus en route to JFK airport. I could live with the unknown of why I persevered with her and was about to win. What was excruciatingly difficult over all was this cab ride to the airport.

I wanted to tell the driver to turn around as her cries for a drink escalated in the back seat. We'd drop Philip and Michelle at any city corner. Dean and I would resume our lives and say we tried to put her on a plane but it was impossible. He'd go back to Rhode Island fueled with a fantastic tale to tell. I'd call Paolo and say Michelle ran away. Her family would believe it. So what if they paid for the cancelled tickets? They should have taken her back.

I turned in my seat to look at Dean. He was staring at me. My protector was now my savior, equally as much as I was Michelle's. There was a profound connection in our eyes, as a sly smile crossed his lips. His head jerked up slightly, directing my attention to the arriving and departing planes at JFK airport that was in front of us. Michelle and Philip were silent as the cab pulled in front of the Alitalia Airline curb stop. When we exited, several people stared at the two well-dressed people and the two who were not.

"You're paying for this horrendous cab ride, too, Michelle. How dare you act up today? I hate you," I said and grabbed my suitcase.

Once inside the terminal, two incidents during check-in convinced me Michelle wanted to go home despite her distasteful behavior and overwhelming fear to face her family.

The first episode occurred at the security checkpoint. Michelle and Dean had their travel documents to present, but I couldn't find my passport. My hands shook. My heart sank. I had visions of the document still on my bureau. Michelle stood over me like a disapproving mother. I handed her things to hold from my purse as I searched frantically.

"It's not here. Go on without me. I'll meet up with you tomorrow," I said and sighed. What else could I do? I'd just blown the whole trip and years of helping her.

"How could you have forgotten your passport?" she shrieked, throwing her hands in the air in disbelief. "I don't want to wait another day to go home."

That emphatic reaction surprised me. Although this trip was difficult to make, it was what she wanted after all. I kept searching through pockets and bags until I found my passport. We proceeded to the check-in counter in silence.

The second incident happened at the check-in counter. I'd grown accustomed to telling Michelle little stories throughout our friendship to keep her attention. Standing at the counter was no exception. As luggage moved along the conveyor, I reminded her when ours was taken we were committed to the flight. If we didn't board, all passengers would deplane and claim their luggage before reboarding.

Dean recalled the time he and I were returning from Madrid. After we taxied onto the runway and readied for take-off, a passenger was asked to identify himself to a flight attendant. No one came forward. The only logical conclusion was he checked his luggage and didn't board.

In a world frightened of bombings, security was extra tight. All passengers left the aircraft and waited three hours on the runway in the hot sun while everyone identified their luggage before reboarding. Michelle was perceptive enough to know what Dean was implying. She should bolt then and not disrupt the flight for hundreds of fellow passengers.

"Do you think I would do that to you after all you have done for me?" she asked him.

As Michelle, Dean and I went through security and ticketing procedures, Philip stood tall, silent and alone beside the rope barrier that separated departing passengers from the general public. His clothes had been on his back for months. His knitted hat was pulled down to his eyebrows. His filthy jeans were loose fitting and had urine stains. His ripped red sneakers were without laces. The motley, wool jacket with the torn plastic patches on the elbows had large food stains. On occasion, his hand went under his armpit to scratch. But that thin rope with Michelle on one side and Philip on the other was symbolic of their past and her future.

Dean and I proceeded to the escalator that would take us to the gate. Michelle must have sensed the final break from Philip and their New York life. She left us abruptly and ran to his side. "Come on, Philip, we're going to have a farewell drink," she said as she reached for his hand to lead him into the secure area.

"Sorry, madam, only boarding passengers can enter here," said an approaching security guard.

"What you talking about, lady?" Michelle said. "We're going to have a drink. Come on, Philip."

The guard quickened her step and looked over her shoulder for additional help.

"Marie," Philip said softly. "You only have 20 minutes. It would be the fastest drink we've ever had. You gotta go, baby. The plane is boarding."

She looked at him in panic. "No, Philip," she sobbed.

"Yes, Marie. You gotta go home."

She rushed into his arms. With the rope between them, they kissed a passionate goodbye. Sighs of grief came out of her as Philip stroked her face. A lingering crowd stared in disbelief, never knowing the tragic story behind that kiss.

I called to Michelle to hurry along, as I stepped on the escalator. I was disgusted and hated her. Dean followed me, motioning for Michelle to step on. She had no choice but to leave Philip's side and walk to the escalator's bottom step. She placed her hands on the moving rails, which slid through her fingers. But her feet were frozen in place as each moving stair approached. She was bent at the waist almost as if an imaginary lasso pulled her backward.

"No. That bitch wouldn't let Philip have a drink with me. Bitch," she screamed into the air.

Dean walked down a few steps and reached for her hand. She took it and stepped onto the escalator. I could only imagine what terrifying thoughts occupied her mind. There was the family to face on the other side. People she had lied to all those years. Life was not fine in America. It was living hell. Steve was dead. She was in horrible condition, only months away from death. Leaving Philip was incredibly traumatic, but leaving the bottle was unbearable.

We reached the top of the escalator. I continued to walk forward hoping my steps would act as a magnet and pull her along. Dean followed. Michelle took several steps forward on the landing. She stopped and turned around as if to run back to Philip. I stopped, too, but for a different reason. Crossing our path was an Alitalia flight attendant leading a line of First Class passengers. They'd been ensconced in an upstairs lounge waiting for special treatment to the gate.

She resembled the Pied Piper; only her mice were Italy's finest. The men were decked out in cashmere coats, carrying Louis Vuitton briefcases, hair slicked back and their shoes shined to the reflection point. The women were equally smashing. They would have passed us by, never raising an eyebrow, except for Michelle's outburst.

"Motherfucker. I want a drink with Philip," she screamed and headed back to the escalator.

Dean turned around instantly. Again, his long legs took him to her faster than she could reach the escalator's top step. He grabbed her by the waist and turned her around. "This way, Michelle," he said and led her away from the moving stairs.

She scuffed her feet and just as she reached the First Class passengers, she brought up a mouthful of saliva and spat on the floor. Several of the ladies gasped. The rest of the line stared at her. She didn't look like a normal passenger about to take an eight-hour flight with them.

As Dean, Michelle and I continued on the long walkway to the gate, Dr. Fischer's departing words repeated in my mind. "Call me when you're boarding," he'd said skeptically. "She loves her addiction, Judith." I never got to make the call.

Michelle stopped at duty-free booths asking for Wild Turkey bourbon but the clerks kept referring her to the next booth. For the last five minutes of Michelle's life in America, she cursed the security guard that refused Philip's entrance. She cursed me. She insisted she'd drink on the plane. That part terrified me. As she approached the opened door of the Alitalia jet, Dean and I nudged her along with encouraging words until she gingerly stepped aboard the aircraft.

<m>

"I want a drink. And I want it now," she said to the stunned flight attendant who showed us to our seats.

"Sit down, Michelle. Let the crew do their job. There are passengers to seat. The overhead bins need to be closed. Shut up," I whispered and glared at her. "You can drink later."

My deep-rooted fear was what would happen to her physically with or without alcohol. A seizure terrified me. What about hallucinations? Sheer drunkenness would put her to sleep if she didn't become belligerent or hysterical. I had to keep her quiet until we were aloft. Only a few more hours and her family would take over. I had had it. If she died, she died. They could bury her. I'd be spared shipping her home in a body bag.

When I went to get a magazine, the flight attendant whom Michelle first encountered about a drink was talking to a colleague in the galley.

"That is her companion," she said pointing at me.

I stopped and faced them.

"Who is she?" the flight attendant asked.

"She's a homeless woman and an alcoholic. She's been hospitalized for eight days and is detoxed. Can you help me so she won't drink a lot?"

"Is she Italian?" she asked with compassion.

"Yes, and I'm taking her home to her family. They haven't seen her in 10 years."

"Who is that man with her?"

"He's my son. Can you help me?"

The flight attendant studied my face. "We'll do our best," she said and smiled.

Dean was stroking Michelle's arm when I returned to my seat. He then opened the airline magazine, turned to the world map and ran his long finger across the flight pattern to Venice, our final destination.

"You're going to love my family. They'll call you *Dino*. You can have anything you want. My cousin is an optometrist. If you or your mother want eyeglasses, just ask," she said.

Dean would later reveal to me that he was disgusted at the airport and knew we had to get her a drink. But the outcome interested him. What would happen to her afterwards? Despite his curiosity, when he buckled his seatbelt, he wanted the journey over. He was proud of her when they said their farewells in New York. She went to the liquor store about six times for Philip, Eugene and Muskrat to celebrate her departure. She never took one drop. Not until it was time to go to the airport did she ask for a drink.

"You're the mother, I'm done," he said when Michelle left her seat for a stroll in the aisle.

Now I had two children to care for on that flight.

It wasn't long before the attendant was at our seat with the drinks' cart. Michelle dug deep into her jean's pocket and pulled out $20.

"I'll have a double Jack Daniels."

The flight attendant looked at me. I nodded yes. What else could I do?

Michelle was given the drink. Dean and I looked at each other, defeated. Within 15 minutes, she wept for Steve. She wept about her family's reaction to her homeless life. She loved us. She loved Philip. She was going back to New York if she didn't like Italy. And on and on and on.

"I left there first class. Now look at me. I'm going home a bum."

She was right about that. Halfway through the flight, she linked arms with Dean and me and kissed our cheeks. She'd never forget what we'd done for her, adding her father and Steve were pulling her home. When the flight attendant passed again, Michelle wanted another drink.

"Sorry, Madam, but we're serving dinner now."

"Motherfucker," Michelle said under her breath. "I'm going to fly TWA next time. You can drink all the time on that airline."

delivered from evil

ONCE MICHELLE'S FEET TOUCHED ITALIAN soil in Milan, the homeless woman who cowered in New York City became self-assured and cocky. She sauntered around the airport scuffing the heels of Dawn's boots on the tile floor as we awaited the flight to Venice. She translated conversations for Dean and me. The fear of meeting her long-lost family diminished whenever she mentioned their upcoming reunion. She took on a bravado I hadn't seen before.

"I'm having a Sambuca. I feel secure now," she declared.

Dean followed her to the bar but I didn't. I was disgusted. She could drink all she wanted. Her alcoholism had beaten me. My responsibility for "Michelle the Drunk" would be over in one hour when we landed in Venice. What difference would another drink make now? Selfish bitch, I thought, as I watched her back when she strolled down the long corridor and entered a bar.

Finally, the flight to Venice boarded. The Sambuca created a remarkably calm Michelle as she sat beside me on the plane. Dean chose a seat at the back. As we neared

Venice and her long-awaited family reunion, she combed her hair and asked to borrow my mascara. It was almost empty, and she complained about that. When she started to talk incessantly, I closed my eyes hoping for a snooze before we landed. Noticing my emotional absence, Michelle got up and sat with Dean.

When we landed and the airplane door opened, a familiar look of terror crossed her face. Inside the terminal, the pounding of the Customs officers' stamps echoed throughout the checkpoint. Michelle handed over her temporary travel document issued by the Italian Consulate in New York. Two officials conferred about its contents and eyed her suspiciously. She glared at them.

My attention was on the large group of people beside the door we'd walk through to exit the area. I pointed them out to Michelle.

"I think that's my brother, Loris," she said squinting at the group. She waved.

The group waved back with arms held high, swaying wildly, looking like a rock concert.

Two Customs guards in full uniform with machine guns poised at their hips, pointing downward, were between Michelle, Dean, me and her waiting family. The guards' faces were expressionless while their eyes surveyed the incoming passengers. As we drew near their inspection table, they instructed us to open our luggage while still on the floor. A drug-sniffing German Shepard dog was summoned.

I'd learn later from Dean that he became terrified with the order. When he opened his suitcase, he could see a slight bulge in the upper half because he'd packed a small plastic bag with marijuana and rolling papers. There was nothing he could do except watch as the dog neared.

"I'd traveled before with a joint in my pants' cuff or tucked somewhere and never got caught. But that was in the States," he told me over a dinner in Venice several nights after our arrival.

"You idiot! We were five minutes away from a miraculous reunion and you've got pot in your suitcase? What were you thinking?"

"I never thought about a drug-sniffing dog at the airport. But I did remember the *Midnight Express* movie and was terrified I'd be in an Italian jail for the rest of my life."

"Everything we endured to get Michelle home and you're about to be arrested for drug possession. Sounds like I had two people with addictions on that trip. How could you do this to me?"

"Ma, I'm not an addict. It was for *relaxation* only. There's a generation gap here. Yours drank. Mine smokes weed. Look, it's obvious I didn't get arrested," he said with a smirk.

"Why not?"

"As I watched the drug dog, I noticed it was nonchalant about the sniffs and only passed over suitcases in front of us. The lady behind me had a small dog in her arms. She put it on the floor to open her suitcase. And when she did, the small dog started to bark. That distracted the drug-sniffing dog enough for it to walk past my suitcase and sniff the other dog. Guess its training wasn't that great or it wasn't trained to sniff out weed."

⟨;m;⟩

After our suitcases and papers were inspected, Michelle, Dean and I passed through the Customs area to one of life's most amazing reunions.

I took a deep breath and faced the door that led to the terminal. At first, Michelle stiffened, but steps from the opened door she slowly raised her arms into the air. Her family surged forward, erupting in joyful screams, yelps and hoots. Michelle glided across the floor, triumphant with her return, resembling a beauty queen parading down the ramp. She wore bloodstained jeans, my white sweater, Greg's leather-trimmed jacket, crack-addict Dawn's leather boots, her hair was disheveled and she was slightly drunk from Sambuca.

"Mireille, Mireille," voices cried out as the crowd rushed toward us. I was terrified by that unknown and wanted to return to New York where she and I were safe. Were those arms permanent? Would they take over for me?

The group separated as Michelle and her mother approached each another. Their steps numbered three, however, for Michelle they covered years of desolation, desperation, inhumane living and a lost life. Michelle collapsed into her mother's outstretched arms. Mrs. Turoldo then took her daughter's face with its broken nose, scars, missing teeth and eyes ringed yellow from alcoholic hepatitis and kissed it on both cheeks.

I watched and felt my head bow in relief. My chin hit my chest in one swoop. A searing flashback to my mother's reaction to my returning Michelle to her mother occurred.

How could she be that cruel to me? Life could be strange and hurtful.

"Judith, *grazie*," whispered an impeccably dressed, blond-haired woman in her early-40s as she approached me. Her deep, translucent-blue eyes matched her sister Michelle's. "Diana," she said as we held each another and wept.

"Franca. *Grazie*, Judith," another sister said, and hugged me as did her brother Loris, Paolo, the nephew who telephoned me, and Cousin Antonio, the family spokesman.

Although engulfed in love from strangers, I was emotionally marooned on an island with Michelle. She wasn't Mireille to me. My eyes followed as other arms encircled her. She floated from one person to another, giddy with her homecoming, finally seeing family faces and not photos. But I couldn't let her go. Her rescuer, me, had become her captive.

An arm turned me around. I faced Mrs. Turoldo who was a stocky woman with rosy cheeks, thick jet-black hair and a lively smile. She wore a black coat, typical of many Italian mothers across the land. Our languages were different, but her strong and penetrating look was universal. My soul shuddered. Her daughter's rescuer, turned her captive at the airport reunion, was transformed into a child in this woman's gaze. My ironclad resolve to bring her daughter home had been granted. Mrs. Turoldo's hands pulled me close to her where I sobbed uncontrollably.

"*Grazie molto*, Judith." She touched my face. She raised her hands. One was complete with five fingers, which she joined with the other hand showing one. Together they made six and represented her children, now together.

Michelle's conversation with her family was in French and Italian, neither of which I understood. I sensed the emotional and humanitarian bond she and I had in New York was dissolving. Dean was baptized "Dino." He, too, was spun like a top and kissed. His six-foot frame towered over everyone. Whenever I glanced at him, my heart was overjoyed. In reliving the event years later, had he been arrested for smuggling marijuana into Italy, the reunion would have been dramatically different.

Cousin Antonio was a dignified gentlemen with a protruding stomach covered with a sweater-vest worn under his tweed sports coat. His round face and balding head had wisps of hair that stuck out over his ears. His gentle, brown eyes were rimmed with glasses.

He whisked Michelle away to the Customs office where she surrendered her travel documents. She was permanently in Italy. She also asked the officials for a martini. Antonio took away her return plane ticket.

Our caravan of automobiles set off for Coderno di Sedegliano, a town in the bucolic hills of northeastern Italy. Dean and I took turns telling Paolo about the grueling journey we'd just made and that Michelle was very ill. He said the family planned to admit her to a 30-day alcoholic rehabilitative hospital close to her mother's home.

The miles whizzed by blurring low farmlands and factories. We passed brick homes with new cars in the driveway and shops. One woman pedaled a bicycle alongside our car at a leisurely speed. She wore a housedress that rested modestly above her knees and high rubber boots. A kerchief was tied under her chin. Another woman skillfully dodged a large pig that had escaped from a pen and was walking nonchalantly on a sidewalk. It was peaceful in the region of Friuli, a far cry from Manhattan. Would Michelle stay here? We finally turned onto a small road and stopped at a signpost with the number three on it. It was the address I used to write to Michelle's mother six weeks' ago.

The two-story, concrete house had a miniscule front yard. A building next door housed thousands of clucking chickens. In the distance, church bells tolled softly from a white steeple. Sonia, Michelle's new sister-in-law, waved us into the house. She was round-shaped and a strawberry-blond with a sweet expressive face. She and Loris, Michelle's youngest brother, lived on the second floor. I recognized them from their wedding picture Michelle kept at Eddie's apartment. She knew some English but her nervousness was evident when she tried to speak it with us.

It was cool inside the neat, pristine home where Michelle once lived. Italian tiles decorated the floors and walls. A kitchen was to the right of the entryway. The dining room, on the left, doubled as the TV area. Dean and I were shown into the dining room where we nervously awaited Michelle and her mother's arrival.

When their car pulled up and stopped, Michelle stepped out and looked at her former home. She wrapped one arm around her mother and the other around Cousin Antonio. They walked up the driveway. More cars arrived and soon the dining room was filled with Turoldo family members. Michelle's nieces and nephews kissed her on both cheeks. They then backed away to stare at their odd aunt from America, the beauty queen, now emaciated, slightly drunk and wearing a sling.

beggar boots to velvet slippers

AFTER THE FAMILY'S INITIAL HELLOS AND stares at Michelle, it was evident a feast was planned to celebrate her homecoming. The family never left the dining room where three oversized chairs with large floral designs lined one wall. A matching couch lined another. A long, blond-wood credenza stretched along the third wall. On it was a TV with a VCR and the family's best china was displayed behind glass doors. An open shelf displayed the photograph of a beautiful, young woman. She had long, blond, shoulder-length hair that was layered to frame her face. Thick bangs almost reached her deep-set eyes that were the same shape as the other women in the room. High cheekbones accentuated a long, narrow nose. Her natural smile revealed beautiful white teeth.

"That's Mireille," Paolo said, noticing me look at the photograph. "It was taken just before she went to America. She'd been crowned Miss San Daniele in a beauty contest. That's her trophy beside the photo."

"*Sì, sì,* Mireille," chimed in her proud mother. She then pointed to a wall with a baby's picture where a cowlick was finger-curled in blond hair. "Mireille," she repeated.

Michelle was seated at the table. Another sister, Augustina, arrived for her tearful reunion. Her eldest brother, Gianpietro, was working in Nigeria and not expected home for several weeks. The sisters hovered over their wayward sibling. One stroked her hair. Another touched her arm. The third held her hand. Mrs. Turoldo stood off to one side and stared at her gaunt daughter with the distended stomach and feeble walk.

Dean and I learned that Michelle and Steve had returned to Coderno di Sedegliano several years into their marriage. He was welcomed by the family, but they noticed he drank all day. Michelle drank, too, but mostly out of the house. Steve didn't want to return to America but Michelle insisted. They drank away most of their money, leaving the family to pay for their return tickets to Houston.

Michelle was described as a rebellious teenager, one who ran off to the discos in Venice, stayed out all night and came home to sleep, only to go out again for more fun. She disregarded her family's concern. Beauty, a good body, good times and big dreams were already tucked into her passport when an American photographer convinced her of fame and fortune in America.

"We begged her not to go," one sister told me through Paolo's translation. "But she was young, packed her bags and left."

At first, she wrote often. But as the years stretched on, letters were returned as "addressee unknown" or the return address had changed. Michelle always said things were fine when the family pressed for answers. She'd telephone her mother, usually collect, telling her she was working in America and life with Steve was wonderful.

Then letters arrived with Eddie Benson's return address. Michelle signed her letters with Eddie's name included, as well as Steve's. She said Eddie helped them. Her mother responded with letters and photos of the family. The letter that informed Michelle of her father's death was sent to Steve's grandmother in Kentucky where it eventually found its way to Eddie's mailbox. What it didn't say was he died surrounded by his family. He never wanted his daughter to go to America and didn't want the family to speak about her in front of him. They knew he was deeply hurt since she was his favorite. They were alike in temperament, including their taste for alcohol. With his last breath, he called out "Mireille" and passed on.

At the reunion dinner table, Michelle spoke to her sisters in French. She spoke to her mother in French and Italian. And to Dean and me, she spoke English. She jumped quickly between languages. I was impressed. But to see her surrounded and touched by her wonderful family was too much for me. I was having flashbacks of her lying in the bank lobby, smelling and lice-ridden. She told me once she only saw feet as she lay on the ground as people stepped over her.

Her family members wore soft sweaters, light wool pants and sleek Italian leather shoes. They were not fabulously rich but I knew they'd pooled their money for her rehabilitation. She was loved and forgiven. That was obvious. But did she love herself enough to recover?

"I want a drink," Michelle said and headed for the kitchen, brushing past Dean and me. She said the same words in Italian. She flung open cabinet doors but her mother had already locked all alcohol in the cellar.

"I want a drink," she said in Italian and rummaged through the shelves.

"No," answered several family members. Her brother, Loris, ran out the door crying. Her sisters' loving looks turned to confusion and fright.

Michelle insisted. She wanted to celebrate her homecoming. She paced the kitchen floor sloughing off the hands that were extended to her. She was brazen, driven, defiant and ugly. The family erupted into emotional words. Hands flew in the air as they spoke. One sister rushed to Michelle to calm her down. Another rushed to her mother who stood confused and dejected. I was equally dismayed, not knowing what to do. I was so exhausted it surprised me I could stand at all.

Dean got up from the dining room table and walked toward Michelle. He turned her around to face him. She looked up and glared at him. He glared back. "What the fuck's going on? You don't need a drink," he said.

"Yes I do. I want to celebrate."

"You wanted to celebrate in New York. Celebrate leaving Philip. Celebrate on the plane. Celebrate in Milan. And now celebrate at home. You're fucking dying, Michelle. How many celebrations are you going to have?"

"You can't stop me," she said.

"You'll have to deal with yourself some time," he told her. "Can't you see what you're doing to your family?"

Mentioning her family did something because she calmed down and returned to the dining room table without a drink. The family was relieved. But I wondered if they realized the sweet, beautiful, young girl of 19 they remembered was now a half-woman, half-animal who kept her addiction well fed from the gutters of New York to their front door.

Only moments after our jubilant reunion in Venice, I questioned what I'd done to the Turoldo family by bringing this wretched, homeless drunk home. Should I have left her to die from acute alcoholism lying beside Philip? Were the memories the family had better than the reality? I thought again about that hypothetical question when Michelle wanted to celebrate her homecoming. But it had no answer. I returned to the dining room table physically and emotionally exhausted. Not only with being awake almost 24 hours, but Michelle was too much for me now.

The homecoming celebration continued on as if nothing had happened. A heaping platter of pencil-thin bread sticks, wrapped with prized San Daniele prosciutto, was passed around. Whiffs of olive oil followed the salad greens passed between outstretched hands just before the macaroni and roasted chicken arrived. There was provolone cheese, bottles of soda and espresso.

Michelle filled her plate, broke bread like a native and was instantly absorbed back into her family. The rapid transformation was amazing to watch. She was part of them. Dean and I were merely guests at her feast, no longer vital to her existence. She'd translate for us and wink on occasion. I spoke enough Spanish to understand the conversation in Italian. Dean was lost.

But it wasn't the feast that captured the moment for him; it was watching Mrs. Turoldo serve us. His eyes followed her. He ate everything she offered. He rubbed his stomach to express his pleasure with her cooking. He smiled continually at her. Everyone could tell she loved him. It was obvious a bond had formed through their eye contact. However, near the end of the dinner, Dean grew profoundly silent and contemplative. His eyes were moist.

"What's wrong Dean? You've changed. Are you sick?"

"No, I'm OK," he said through a hoarse whisper. "I've just discovered my roots, Mom. This is where I come from. Michelle's mother is my Grandma we used to visit every Sunday back home before she died. The food, even down to the tablecloth and all the relatives around the table, is how I grew up."

Watching Michelle's mother reminded him of his lost youth. He missed those Sunday afternoons when the water was boiling and the handmade spaghetti was being rolled out, cut into strips and dropped into the pot. In spite of me being Irish, I'd assumed my husband's Italian culture and our children were raised with many Italian traditions. I knew exactly what he was talking about. Michelle's mother was an exact duplicate of Dean's Italian grandmother, right down to the way she sat on a chair with her legs apart.

Little did Dean know when he stooped so low on a New York street to help Michelle raise her dignity to higher ground that he'd discover the depths of his Italian background through her family in Coderno di Sedegliano. It was quite a revelation for him.

As we prepared to leave Mrs. Turoldo's home to over-night at Diana's, also home to Paolo who could translate for us, the reunion was still in progress. Michelle had changed into a soft, slinky, pink robe. Her feet were shod in new, black velvet slippers with gold crests. When I looked at them, my mind flashbacked to her filthy red boots that I always looked for when the homeless were huddled and non-recognizable. Instantly, I decided Michelle Browning was dead. Marie was dead, too. The young woman in the velvet slippers was Mireille Turoldo.

"Miré," I said, as her nickname rolled off my tongue. It was the name used by the family. We were at her front door hugging goodbye. "You'll never again be Michelle Browning or Marie. Both of those women are dead. You're Miré to me now."

⟨:m:⟩

Within the hour, Dean and I arrived at Diana's contemporary home where we met her husband, Guerrino. He was a handsome, charming man with an easy smile, effervescent personality and ruddy complexion. He loved fishing. On quiet nights he sat at a desk in the dining room twisting feathers and twine into lures. He could build and repair anything but in the summer months, he pushed a *gelato* cart on the beach. That's how he met his wife, and they continued to act like sweethearts. There was a younger son, Favio, who attended a boarding school. Paolo was a baker

Diana and Loris, Mireille Turoldo's siblings, Italy, March 1991

at the renowned Harry's Bar in Venice but was laid off and waiting for the tourists to return after the Gulf War slump.

We were shown to an apartment on an upper floor. That night Dean and I told the family what we knew about Miré's life in New York, although the Turoldo family had decided Miré would never return to America. They couldn't imagine begging with a cup. Philip's $1,000 insurance money and sleeping on the bank floor was revealed. They asked about Eddie Benson, transfixed by the sordid details.

I was curious about Paolo's visit to America. What had he seen? Was Eddie telling the truth? Why didn't someone from the family take Miré home before I reached out to them?

He told Dean and me that he visited America and New York City for the first time in August 1990. His grandmother had given him Eddie's address. He remembered his Aunt Mireille as someone who played with him in Coderno di Sedegliano when he was a small boy.

"So I go with this address and see people sleeping in the streets and pushing shopping carts," he said in halting English.

He rang Eddie's doorbell but no answer. Someone else entered the building and let him in. He was frightened when he saw the dark hallway but he entered anyway. He climbed the five flights of stairs and knocked on Eddie's door. No answer.

The next day he returned, still terrified, but he didn't carry any money. He was let in again by someone sitting on the stoop, and he climbed the stairs to Eddie's apartment. This time he was home. When Paolo saw the condition of the apartment, he was very frightened. How could his aunt live there? What was going on? America confused him. When Eddie learned who Paolo was, he took him to find his aunt.

"This is Mireille," Eddie said, pointing to a woman drunk and asleep in the subway station.

Paolo recognized only her eyes. They were the same blue and shape as those of his family in Italy. She showed no emotion when he said he was Paolo, her nephew from Italy. He remembered thinking what is wrong with her husband that he cannot take care of his wife. She took him to a street corner where he met Philip and Eugene. He was stunned when she took a bottle of alcohol from them and drank most of it. She then took him to meet Steve who was on the ground in the subway station, but she had to hold his head up for him to say hello. Paolo asked his aunt if everything was all right. What was happening? She said life was fine. She was happy.

"I began to cry talking to her. I didn't know what to do," he said still confused by the situation. Before returning to Italy, he went back to Eddie's house but no one answered the doorbell.

"I told my parents, but if you don't see, you don't believe," he said. He never told his grandmother, Miré's mother.

When my letter to Mrs. Turoldo arrived with the shocking photograph of Miré, it was painfully clear what had become of her daughter. But my words were in English and needed a perfect translation. She made the all-day trip to Rome to show it to her cousin, Antonio. He gave it to an English professor to translate. Mrs. Turoldo and Antonio returned to Coderno di Sedegliano and consulted with the regional bishop. He was a cousin to Miré's father.

The family decided she'd be brought home and cured, if possible. Mrs. Turoldo didn't eat or sleep for three days. Distraught and confused, she placed my letter in the church down the road and waited. The family chose Paolo to talk to me. But who would bring Mireille home? Mrs. Turoldo was frightened of America. And how would any family member work with the American authorities to get Mireille a passport? The task seemed insurmountable with time running out. She continued to pray and awaited Miré's telephone call saying she wanted to go home. When it came, the answer was clear that she did. And when I suggested taking her, Mrs. Turoldo's prayers were answered.

.

i'll miss
her smile

SAN DANIELE IS KNOWN FOR THE BEST prosciutto in the land. But the alcoholic soul is nourished in a peaceful hospital set back from the main road. If Miré was to be cured, it would be in this hospital. She spent the weekend with her mother and kept asking for a drink. The family called the hospital and was advised to give her a little from time to time. They did, and she settled down.

Paolo drove Dean and me to his grandmother's home on the day Miré was to be admitted to the hospital. When we entered the home, although Miré was in good humor, she wasn't ready to leave. She took me into her former bedroom where her mother was ironing a few nightgowns for her hospital stay. She asked me, through Miré's translation, to help her daughter get dressed.

I pulled on her new stretch pants. A new white sweater slipped easily over her head. I adjusted the sling for her arm. Together, we removed the sponge curlers in her hair. When I glanced at Mrs. Turoldo, she was watching her daughter and me. She had to see our common love and friendship.

"Are you happy now?" I asked her in Spanish, which I knew was close enough to Italian.

Miré translated her answer. "She said she's now content knowing where her six children are. But she wants to know what took you so long to contact her? Why did you pass me on the street for two years and do nothing?"

I couldn't answer, only lower my head and hold back a sob. Miré and her mother rushed to my side with a hug. The subject was dropped.

Mireille's bedroom had remained unchanged through the years she'd been away. The blond-wood bedroom set had a large armoire in one corner and a double bed against one wall. Draped across the headboard was a miniature rug with a picture of Pope John Paul stamped on it. In Miré's absence, the room was used to iron, sew and for storage.

The day Miré readied herself for the hospital, the portable tape recorder beside the bed blared *The Doors* tape Dean bought her for the trip home. Mrs. Turoldo covered her ears in jest, smiled and returned to her ironing. Miré took a long shoehorn and slid her feet into the black velvet slippers. When she stood up, she wobbled. The stretch pants bagged in the seat. She looked in the mirror and grabbed a razor to shave her upper lip.

"Don't do that. You'll end up with a full-fledged mustache," I said and cringed.

"Sorry but I'm doing it," she said and proceeded to shave.

She blew her nose with a cotton handkerchief remembering that she used to use a newspaper found on the street. Just before we slipped Greg's knitted jacket over her shoul-

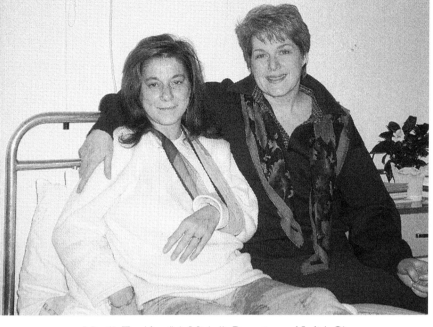

Mireille Turoldo a/k/a Michelle Browning and Judith Glynn,
Alcohol rehab hospital in Italy, March 1991

der, I suggested I cut off the Roosevelt Hospital identifica-
tion band she still wore. She agreed but wanted to keep it.

Waiting for our arrival at the hospital with hugs, kisses
and words of encouragement were Miré's sisters, several of
their children, Paolo, Loris and Cousin Antonio. We sat
in a large open room used as a dining room, meeting hall
and recreation center. The walls were covered with alcohol-
ism-recovery posters. While we waited for Miré to be admitted, Franca gave her sister a photograph.

Stretched out on a blanket in a park-like setting were
Steve and Miré. She wore shorts and a halter top, both of
which accentuated her wonderful body. Leaning on his elbow beside her was Steve, a muscular, dark-haired, hand-

some young man who was a dead ringer for Burt Reynolds, mustache and all.

"That's Steve and me in Texas," Miré said wistfully.

She stared at the picture while large tears rolled down her cheeks and dropped on Greg's jacket, which she continued to wear in Italy. Franca pulled out a tissue for her sister and one for herself.

"Mireille Turoldo," the admitting nurse called out.

The entire family followed Miré and the woman into a large room. Seated at a table was a serious-looking young doctor wearing horn-rimmed glasses. He had a shadow of a beard, and wore a white doctor's coat over his elegant clothing. Beside him was a young woman we'd later learn was the hospital psychiatrist. The family sat on soft canvas directors' chairs scattered about the room.

"Sit beside me," Miré said to me when she approached the doctor's table.

Dean pulled a chair over for me and one for himself.

"These papers say I'll be treated for my alcohol addiction, put on an exercise program, my nose and teeth will be fixed and I'll be given a proper diet to eliminate my anemia," she told me.

"Sounds good to me, Miré."

After a few words between the doctor and Miré, she leaned over to me and said softly, "He wants to know what happened in America."

"Tell him everything."

She listed what she drank and how much she could consume in a ten-minute span. Then her drug history was revealed, which was taken orally and intravenously for two

Top: Dean Albanese, Mireille Turoldo and Cousin Paolo, Alcohol rehab hospital in Italy, March 1991

Above: Dean Albanese and Franca (Mireille's sister). Italy – March 1991

Above right: Mireille Turoldo and Cousin Antonio

Right: Mrs. Maria Turoldo, Augustina, (Mireille's sister) and unidentified child

years before switching exclusively to alcohol. Her family leaned forward in their chairs, listening intently with pained expressions.

"The doctor wants me to stay for 30 days. I thought it would be two weeks," she translated for me.

"What difference does it make? Stop being difficult."

"I'm used to living on the streets, not being cooped up. Thirty days is impossible. I'm not staying."

"This is your last chance to live," the doctor told her. "You're finished with alcohol."

I motioned to Franca that I wanted the photograph of Steve and Miré. She rummaged in her pocketbook and gave it to me. The room was silent when I shoved it in front of Miré.

"Look at this," I screamed. I was furious. "Ask Steve if he wants 30 more days. What do you think is his answer?" I glared at her. "Thirty more days or death for you. For me, it doesn't matter anymore. Die, bitch. It's your life to do as you please."

She was seething but continued to look at the photograph. Her shoulders slumped, her leg stopped swinging. "I'll stay," she answered dejectedly. "I have no choice."

Within minutes, Miré and I were in a tiny room where she undressed for an examination and was quickly taken to her hospital room. When a nurse appeared and announced an upcoming Alcoholics Anonymous meeting, Miré didn't want to attend. She relented with pressure from the family. Five minutes into the meeting, she bolted from her seat, announcing over her shoulder she was leaving the hospital. She was going back to New York and Philip. And as he'd done many times before, Dean followed, grabbed her elbow and guided her back to her chair.

For the next week, Dean and I were entertained by the Turoldo family. We took long countryside rides through Italy; we were driven to Austria; we walked in Venice; had dinner visits at the homes of Miré's sisters and were taken to see her in the hospital. She was usually sedated. When she wasn't, we argued heavily about her staying in the hospital. Our friendship was breaking as we grew apart.

The morning I packed to leave Miré and Italy, it was difficult. I'd miss her in my life. We'd been through so much. Then there was the realization she might return to drinking after 30 days' rehab, but that wasn't my problem anymore. Maybe I should have let her die in the gutter versus presenting her to her family, now shackled with her addiction. But I believed in destiny, hope and the ability to change a destroyed life into one worth living. That voice I heard throughout our odyssey whispered to me that I had done the right thing.

Miré held my hand when she walked me down the hospital staircase. Dean trailed. We were going to the airport. It was so hard to say goodbye to her. I ached all over.

"Don't die, Miré," I whispered, as I hugged her frail, anemic body. "Go on to become a beautiful, fulfilled woman. And remember that I love you. We will stay in touch forever. I promise."

"What am I going to do here without you? Thank you, Judith, for all you did." She looked down and not at me.

I nodded but wanted more than her gratitude. We'd shared a divine gift, given for mystical reasons. Her thank you wasn't enough. "Recreate this deed with someone else when you're well," I said and cupped her face.

She nodded her head in agreement but couldn't speak. Miré hugged Dean goodbye and kissed him on both cheeks. Farewell words were spoken with their eyes.

Mrs. Turoldo stood nearby. When a cool breeze sent a shudder through her daughter's body, she took her hand and led her toward the hospital's entrance. A flicker of terror crossed Miré's eyes as she walked backward, keeping us in her sight. Dean gave her the thumbs-up sign. She returned it. He then put his arm around my shoulder and we walked away.

epilogue

MIREILLE TUROLDO'S PUBLIC HOMECOMING turned
into an embarrassing article in the regional newspaper. Lo-
cal beauty queen becomes a homeless drunk in New York
City. One photo showed Mireille as Miss San Daniele and
another showed her in a hospital bed with her mother at
her side.

When Miré and I began to write letters, mine were
inspirational and optimistic about her new life. One letter
from Miré boasted she'd been sober for three months. Another thanked me for saving her life. Another said she was
bored in Coderno di Sedegliano. She'd told her mother she
didn't want to live there. Please ask Philip to finance her return ticket. She'd look for work in New York. Please contact
Steve's parents because she needed to prove her marriage to
get a passport.

My letters voiced strong objections. I brushed off con-
tacting Steve's parents. I'd spoken to Philip, still on the
street. His relationship with her was over. She was to stay
in Italy and forget about him. Sightings of Eugene became

Italian newspaper article about Mireille, March, 1991

sporadic as well. Only Muskrat cried when I mentioned her name, confessing to me how much he loved Michelle.

Dean didn't continue his relationship with Miré either. If she'd call me, I'd patch him in on a conference call. We'd talk about the past but never a future meeting. That confused her since she loved him. But he'd already distanced himself from her, New York, Italy and the remarkable deed he'd accomplished.

But Miré kept up her contact with me, her only New York link. Eventually, she wrote she was in love with an American serviceman from nearby Aviano Air Force base. The letter included photos of them traveling and others of her lying seductively in front of a fireplace. Each photo of her was more beautiful than the last.

Halfway through my odyssey with Michelle to Marie to Miré, I began to write our story. The release helped me grasp the topsy-turvy ride we'd taken. After Italy, the finished manuscript was put in a drawer. I didn't want to exploit her or our journey with its publication. My mother's assumption that she was only a subject for me never dimmed.

One day, Miré called to say she was moving to America with her new American boyfriend. They'd stop in New York to see me. I didn't ask details but somehow she was able to leave Italy with him. When she rang my doorbell from the street, I was extremely nervous as the elevator inched upward to my floor. She barely knocked on my door, as I flung it open. Before me, Miré stood as a stunning woman. Her long, wavy blond hair rested on her shoulders. Her teeth were straight and white. Her translucent blue eyes were bright and knowing. Her body had transformed into a voluptuous beauty. She was sober, talkative, sexy and full of joy. She helped me cook dinner for the three of us.

I liked her boyfriend immediately, although we weren't strangers. He'd written to thank me for saving Miré. They'd met when he picked her up as she hitchhiked out of her hometown. She'd detoxed twice since they'd been living together. He felt she needed to open up with someone. It was important for me to know he wasn't taking advantage of her. They married in Tennessee in November 1994.

I was overjoyed with the new Miré. The cards, letters and calls that came from her new American home revealed a love of life and a woman learning the computer. She rode horses at a stable near the military base. She swam in a pool. Photos revealed a nice home, complete with two dogs, and a cruise taken with her husband's parents.

But the dark side of Miré hovered, so I'd learn from her husband's distraught letter to me. She destroyed his heart and their marriage by drinking heavily again. He had her sent back to Italy. I never contacted Miré when I learned that fact, nor did she contact me. Whenever I saw Philip, Eugene and Muskrat in the neighborhood, I'd always stop and talk to them. Passersby would stop and look at me wondering how I could do it. In time, however, my homeless friends began to disappear one by one. I assumed death claimed them.

My life in New York City continued on, eclectic as ever. I started a successful Web-based business and bought real estate but I'd stopped writing, backing off from the craft I loved. I had a few boyfriends, but chose to maintain a single lifestyle over marriage.

My relationship with my mother improved when my daughter planned her marriage. She wanted reconciliation so I relented, telling Mother we'd never again be mother and daughter. We were adult women, and I wanted to be treated that way. Her last years were spent in a nursing home where I was dutiful and loving until her end.

Years passed before a routine physical for an insurance policy revealed the deadly hepatitis C virus still growing inside me for over 20 years. What had been named chronic non-A, non-B hepatitis was finally isolated as type C. Although my genotype was not as serious as others, I chose to endure a grueling six-month treatment, which failed.

Determined to succeed, I underwent a second six-month round, which was successful.

My children blossomed in adulthood. Three remained in Rhode Island. Greg became a talented crane operator. Dean continued on with carpentry, preferring a quiet life in a Rhode Island town. To this day, he keeps a photo of Miré on his refrigerator. Lesley married the man she loved and is a best friend to me. Derek never returned to his home state, choosing to live in New York City where he succeeded in the finance world. They'd present me with six grandchildren to dote upon. To do that, I purchased a home in Providence, riding back in on my triumphant white horse, dividing my time with New York.

Always pining to write and after decades of published travel articles, I finally tackled a novel. But I wasn't prepared for the creative loss at its publication. To fill the void, I took out the faded Michelle and me manuscript, immediately moved by its intensity. But with her silence after many years, I knew its ending.

A call to her family in 2013 confirmed Miré died in 1998 at age 42. She'd moved to Magnano, miles from her village. A neighbor found her dead in bed. Death was caused by an esophageal hemorrhage. I didn't need details, only that she had an excellent and loving relationship with her family.

Someday I'll visit Miré's gravesite. It's the least I can do. I was an ordinary woman until she transformed me into a fearless one who accomplished an extraordinary deed in life. In the end, Miré died with dignity, not in a New York City gutter, for which I'm grateful. That's all I ever wanted.

Mireille Turoldo in Judith Glynn's apartment, New York, NY, June 1995

ABOUT THE AUTHOR

Judith Glynn began her writing life many years ago with a travel article about Ireland. Once published, she went on to publish hundreds of articles over the years, many for national newspapers and more recently for the Web. Her first novel, *A Collector of Affections: Tales from a Woman's Heart* entwines romance with travel for the middle-aged reader. She lives in New York, Rhode Island and settles in quickly in the newest destination.

Made in the USA
Columbia, SC
07 January 2023

74586036R00104